OECD Guidelines for Multinational Enterprises 2011 Edition

OECD

This work is published on the responsibility of the Secretary-General of the OECD. The opinions expressed and arguments employed herein do not necessarily reflect the official views of the Organisation or of the governments of its member countries.

Please cite this publication as:
OECD (2011), *OECD Guidelines for Multinational Enterprises*, OECD Publishing.
http://dx.doi.org/10.1787/9789264115415-en

ISBN 978-92-64-11528-6 (print)
ISBN 978-92-64-11541-5 (PDF)

Corrigenda to OECD publications may be found on line at: *www.oecd.org/publishing/corrigenda*.

Foreword

The *OECD Guidelines for Multinational Enterprises* are recommendations addressed by governments to multinational enterprises operating in or from adhering countries. They provide non-binding principles and standards for responsible business conduct in a global context consistent with applicable laws and internationally recognised standards. The *Guidelines* are the only multilaterally agreed and comprehensive code of responsible business conduct that governments have committed to promoting.

The *Guidelines'* recommendations express the shared values of the governments of countries from which a large share of international direct investment originates and which are home to many of the largest multinational enterprises. The *Guidelines* aim to promote positive contributions by enterprises to economic, environmental and social progress worldwide.

The *Guidelines* are supported by a unique implementation mechanism of National Contact Points (NCPs), agencies established by adhering governments to promote and implement the *Guidelines*. The NCPs assist enterprises and their stakeholders to take appropriate measures to further the implementation of the *Guidelines*. They also provide a mediation and conciliation platform for resolving practical issues that may arise.

On 4 May 2010, the governments of the 42 OECD and non-OECD countries adhering to the OECD Declaration on International Investment and Multinational Enterprises and related Decision started work on updating the *Guidelines* to reflect changes in the landscape for international investment and multinational enterprises since the last review in 2000. The changes agreed aim to ensure the continued role of the *Guidelines* as a leading international instrument for the promotion of responsible business conduct.

The updated *Guidelines* and the related Decision were adopted by the 42 adhering governments on 25 May 2011 at the OECD's 50th Anniversary Ministerial Meeting.

Changes to the *Guidelines* include:

- A new human rights chapter, which is consistent with the Guiding Principles on Business and Human Rights: Implementing the United Nations "Protect, Respect and Remedy" Framework.

- A new and comprehensive approach to due diligence and responsible supply chain management representing significant progress relative to earlier approaches.
- Important changes in many specialised chapters, such as on Employment and Industrial Relations; Combating Bribery, Bribe Solicitation and Extortion, Environment, Consumer Interests, Disclosure and Taxation.
- Clearer and reinforced procedural guidance to strengthen the role of the NCPs, improve their performance and foster functional equivalence.
- A pro-active implementation agenda to assist enterprises in meeting their responsibilities as new challenges arise.

The Update of the *Guidelines* was conducted by the adhering governments and included intensive consultations with a wide range of stakeholders and partners. All non-adhering G20 countries were invited to participate on an equal footing; they made important contributions, as did participants in the regional consultations in Asia, Africa, Latin America and the Middle East and North Africa. The OECD Business and Industry Advisory Committee, the OECD Trade Union Advisory Committee and OECD Watch represented the views of business, workers' organisations and non-governmental organisations (NGOs) through regular consultation meetings and their active participation in the Advisory Group of the Chair of the Working Party responsible for the Update of the *Guidelines*. The UN Secretary-General's Special Representative on Business and Human Rights, Professor John Ruggie, the International Labour Organisation together with other international organisations, also provided extensive input on the Update.

OECD committees on Competition; Consumer Policy; Corporate Governance; Employment, Labour and Social Affairs; Environment Policy; Fiscal Affairs; and the Working Group on Bribery in International Business Transactions contributed to the revisions of the relevant specialised chapters of the *Guidelines*.

The work on the Update was supported by the Investment Division as Secretariat of the OECD Investment Committee, in close collaboration with the Legal Directorate; the Centre for Tax Policy and Administration; the Anti-Corruption Division; the Competition Division; the Corporate Affairs Division; the Division for Employment Analysis and Policy; the Environment and Economy Integration Division; and the Information, Communications and Consumer Policy Division.

Table of Contents

DECLARATION ON INTERNATIONAL INVESTMENT AND MULTINATIONAL ENTERPRISES

25 May 2011

ADHERING GOVERNMENTS[1]

CONSIDERING:

- That international investment is of major importance to the world economy, and has considerably contributed to the development of their countries;

- That multinational enterprises play an important role in this investment process;

- That international co-operation can improve the foreign investment climate, encourage the positive contribution which multinational enterprises can make to economic, social and environmental progress, and minimise and resolve difficulties which may arise from their operations;

- That the benefits of international co-operation are enhanced by addressing issues relating to international investment and multinational enterprises through a balanced framework of inter-related instruments;

1. As at 25 May 2011 adhering governments are those of all OECD members, as well as Argentina, Brazil, Egypt, Latvia, Lithuania, Morocco, Peru and Romania. The European Community has been invited to associate itself with the section on National Treatment on matters falling within its competence.

DECLARE:

Guidelines for Multinational Enterprises	I.	That they jointly recommend to multinational enterprises operating in or from their territories the observance of the Guidelines, set forth in Annex 1 hereto[2], having regard to the considerations and understandings that are set out in the Preface and are an integral part of them;”
National Treatment	II. 1.	That adhering governments should, consistent with their needs to maintain public order, to protect their essential security interests and to fulfil commitments relating to international peace and security, accord to enterprises operating in their territories and owned or controlled directly or indirectly by nationals of another adhering government (hereinafter referred to as "Foreign-Controlled Enterprises") treatment under their laws, regulations and administrative practices, consistent with international law and no less favourable than that accorded in like situations to domestic enterprises (hereinafter referred to as "National Treatment");
	2.	That adhering governments will consider applying "National Treatment" in respect of countries other than adhering governments;
	3.	That adhering governments will endeavour to ensure that their territorial subdivisions apply "National Treatment";
	4.	That this Declaration does not deal with the right of adhering governments to regulate the entry of foreign investment or the conditions of establishment of foreign enterprises;

2. The text of the *Guidelines for Multinational Enterprises* is reproduced in Part I of this publication.

Conflicting Requirements	III.	That they will co-operate with a view to avoiding or minimising the imposition of conflicting requirements on multinational enterprises and that they will take into account the general considerations and practical approaches as set forth in Annex 2 hereto[3].
International Investment Incentives and Disincentives	IV. 1.	That they recognise the need to strengthen their co-operation in the field of international direct investment;
	2.	That they thus recognise the need to give due weight to the interests of adhering governments affected by specific laws, regulations and administrative practices in this field (hereinafter called "measures") providing official incentives and disincentives to international direct investment;
	3.	That adhering governments will endeavour to make such measures as transparent as possible, so that their importance and purpose can be ascertained and that information on them can be readily available;
Consultation Procedures	V.	That they are prepared to consult one another on the above matters in conformity with the relevant Decisions of the Council;
Review	VI.	That they will review the above matters periodically with a view to improving the effectiveness of international economic co-operation among adhering governments on issues relating to international investment and multinational enterprises.

3. The text of General Considerations and Practical Approaches concerning Conflicting Requirements Imposed on Multinational Enterprises is available from the OECD Website *www.oecd.org/daf/investment.*

Part I

OECD Guidelines for Multinational Enterprises

Recommendations for responsible business conduct in a global context

Text and Commentary

Note by the Secretariat: The commentaries on the *OECD Guidelines for Multinational Enterprises* have been adopted by the Investment Committee in enlarged session, including the eight non-Member adherents* to the *Declaration on International Investment and Multinational Enterprises*, to provide information on and explanation of the text of the *Guidelines for Multinational Enterprises* and of the Council Decision on the *OECD Guidelines for Multinational Enterprises*. They are not part of the *Declaration on International Investment and Multinational Enterprises* or of the Council Decision on the *OECD Guidelines for Multinational Enterprises*.

In this publication, the commentaries are placed after the chapter they refer to and are numbered consecutively from 1 to 106.

* Argentina, Brazil, Egypt, Latvia, Lithuania, Morocco, Peru and Romania.

Preface

1. The *OECD Guidelines for Multinational Enterprises* (the *Guidelines*) are recommendations addressed by governments to multinational enterprises. The *Guidelines* aim to ensure that the operations of these enterprises are in harmony with government policies, to strengthen the basis of mutual confidence between enterprises and the societies in which they operate, to help improve the foreign investment climate and to enhance the contribution to sustainable development made by multinational enterprises. The *Guidelines* are part of the *OECD Declaration on International Investment and Multinational Enterprises* the other elements of which relate to national treatment, conflicting requirements on enterprises, and international investment incentives and disincentives. The *Guidelines* provide voluntary principles and standards for responsible business conduct consistent with applicable laws and internationally recognised standards. However, the countries adhering to the *Guidelines* make a binding commitment to implement them in accordance with the *Decision of the OECD Council on the OECD Guidelines for Multinational Enterprises*. Furthermore, matters covered by the *Guidelines* may also be the subject of national law and international commitments.

2. International business has experienced far-reaching structural change and the *Guidelines* themselves have evolved to reflect these changes. With the rise of service and knowledge-intensive industries and the expansion of the Internet economy, service and technology enterprises are playing an increasingly important role in the international marketplace. Large enterprises still account for a major share of international investment, and there is a trend toward large-scale international mergers. At the same time, foreign investment by small- and medium-sized enterprises has also increased and these enterprises now play a significant role on the international scene. Multinational enterprises, like their domestic counterparts, have evolved to encompass a broader range of business arrangements and organisational forms. Strategic alliances and closer relations with suppliers and contractors tend to blur the boundaries of the enterprise.

3. The rapid evolution in the structure of multinational enterprises is also reflected in their operations in the developing world, where foreign direct investment has grown rapidly. In developing countries, multinational enterprises have diversified beyond primary production and extractive industries into manufacturing, assembly, domestic market development and services. Another key development is the emergence of multinational enterprises based in developing countries as major international investors.

4. The activities of multinational enterprises, through international trade and investment, have strengthened and deepened the ties that join the countries and regions of the world. These activities bring substantial benefits to home and host countries. These benefits accrue when multinational enterprises supply the products and services that consumers want to buy at competitive prices and when they provide fair returns to suppliers of capital. Their trade and investment activities contribute to the efficient use of capital, technology and human and natural resources. They facilitate the transfer of technology among the regions of the world and the development of technologies that reflect local conditions. Through both formal training and on-the-job learning enterprises also promote the development of human capital and creating employment opportunities in host countries.

5. The nature, scope and speed of economic changes have presented new strategic challenges for enterprises and their stakeholders. Multinational enterprises have the opportunity to implement best practice policies for sustainable development that seek to ensure coherence between economic, environmental and social objectives. The ability of multinational enterprises to promote sustainable development is greatly enhanced when trade and investment are conducted in a context of open, competitive and appropriately regulated markets.

6. Many multinational enterprises have demonstrated that respect for high standards of business conduct can enhance growth. Today's competitive forces are intense and multinational enterprises face a variety of legal, social and regulatory settings. In this context, some enterprises may be tempted to neglect appropriate principles and standards of conduct in an attempt to gain undue competitive advantage. Such practices by the few may call into question the reputation of the many and may give rise to public concerns.

7. Many enterprises have responded to these public concerns by developing internal programmes, guidance and management systems that underpin their commitment to good corporate citizenship, good practices and good business and employee conduct. Some of them have

called upon consulting, auditing and certification services, contributing to the accumulation of expertise in these areas. Enterprises have also promoted social dialogue on what constitutes responsible business conduct and have worked with stakeholders, including in the context of multi-stakeholder initiatives, to develop guidance for responsible business conduct. The *Guidelines* clarify the shared expectations for business conduct of the governments adhering to them and provide a point of reference for enterprises and for other stakeholders. Thus, the *Guidelines* both complement and reinforce private efforts to define and implement responsible business conduct.

8. Governments are co-operating with each other and with other actors to strengthen the international legal and policy framework in which business is conducted. The start of this process can be dated to the work of the International Labour Organisation in the early twentieth century. The adoption by the United Nations in 1948 of the Universal Declaration of Human Rights was another landmark event. It was followed by the ongoing development of standards relevant for many areas of responsible business conduct – a process that continues to this day. The OECD has contributed in important ways to this process through the development of standards covering such areas as the environment, the fight against corruption, consumer interests, corporate governance and taxation.

9. The common aim of the governments adhering to the *Guidelines* is to encourage the positive contributions that multinational enterprises can make to economic, environmental and social progress and to minimise the difficulties to which their various operations may give rise. In working towards this goal, governments find themselves in partnership with the many businesses, trade unions and other non-governmental organisations that are working in their own ways toward the same end. Governments can help by providing effective domestic policy frameworks that include stable macroeconomic policy, non-discriminatory treatment of enterprises, appropriate regulation and prudential supervision, an impartial system of courts and law enforcement and efficient and honest public administration. Governments can also help by maintaining and promoting appropriate standards and policies in support of sustainable development and by engaging in ongoing reforms to ensure that public sector activity is efficient and effective. Governments adhering to the *Guidelines* are committed to continuous improvement of both domestic and international policies with a view to improving the welfare and living standards of all people.

I. Concepts and Principles

1. The *Guidelines* are recommendations jointly addressed by governments to multinational enterprises. They provide principles and standards of good practice consistent with applicable laws and internationally recognised standards. Observance of the *Guidelines* by enterprises is voluntary and not legally enforceable. Nevertheless, some matters covered by the *Guidelines* may also be regulated by national law or international commitments.

2. Obeying domestic laws is the first obligation of enterprises. The *Guidelines* are not a substitute for nor should they be considered to override domestic law and regulation. While the *Guidelines* extend beyond the law in many cases, they should not and are not intended to place an enterprise in situations where it faces conflicting requirements. However, in countries where domestic laws and regulations conflict with the principles and standards of the *Guidelines*, enterprises should seek ways to honour such principles and standards to the fullest extent which does not place them in violation of domestic law.

3. Since the operations of multinational enterprises extend throughout the world, international co-operation in this field should extend to all countries. Governments adhering to the *Guidelines* encourage the enterprises operating on their territories to observe the *Guidelines* wherever they operate, while taking into account the particular circumstances of each host country.

4. A precise definition of multinational enterprises is not required for the purposes of the *Guidelines*. These enterprises operate in all sectors of the economy. They usually comprise companies or other entities established in more than one country and so linked that they may co-ordinate their operations in various ways. While one or more of these entities may be able to exercise a significant influence over the activities of others, their degree of autonomy within the enterprise may vary widely from one multinational enterprise to another. Ownership may be private, State or mixed. The *Guidelines* are addressed to all the entities within the multinational enterprise (parent companies and/or local entities). According to the actual distribution of responsibilities among

them, the different entities are expected to co-operate and to assist one another to facilitate observance of the *Guidelines*.

5. The *Guidelines* are not aimed at introducing differences of treatment between multinational and domestic enterprises; they reflect good practice for all. Accordingly, multinational and domestic enterprises are subject to the same expectations in respect of their conduct wherever the *Guidelines* are relevant to both.

6. Governments wish to encourage the widest possible observance of the *Guidelines*. While it is acknowledged that small- and medium-sized enterprises may not have the same capacities as larger enterprises, governments adhering to the *Guidelines* nevertheless encourage them to observe the *Guidelines'* recommendations to the fullest extent possible.

7. Governments adhering to the *Guidelines* should not use them for protectionist purposes nor use them in a way that calls into question the comparative advantage of any country where multinational enterprises invest.

8. Governments have the right to prescribe the conditions under which multinational enterprises operate within their jurisdictions, subject to international law. The entities of a multinational enterprise located in various countries are subject to the laws applicable in these countries. When multinational enterprises are subject to conflicting requirements by adhering countries or third countries, the governments concerned are encouraged to co-operate in good faith with a view to resolving problems that may arise.

9. Governments adhering to the *Guidelines* set them forth with the understanding that they will fulfil their responsibilities to treat enterprises equitably and in accordance with international law and with their contractual obligations.

10. The use of appropriate international dispute settlement mechanisms, including arbitration, is encouraged as a means of facilitating the resolution of legal problems arising between enterprises and host country governments.

11. Governments adhering to the *Guidelines* will implement them and encourage their use. They will establish National Contact Points that promote the *Guidelines* and act as a forum for discussion of all matters relating to the *Guidelines*. The adhering Governments will also participate in appropriate review and consultation procedures to address issues concerning interpretation of the *Guidelines* in a changing world.

II. General Policies

Enterprises should take fully into account established policies in the countries in which they operate, and consider the views of other stakeholders. In this regard:

A. Enterprises should:

1. Contribute to economic, environmental and social progress with a view to achieving sustainable development.
2. Respect the internationally recognised human rights of those affected by their activities.
3. Encourage local capacity building through close co-operation with the local community, including business interests, as well as developing the enterprise's activities in domestic and foreign markets, consistent with the need for sound commercial practice.
4. Encourage human capital formation, in particular by creating employment opportunities and facilitating training opportunities for employees.
5. Refrain from seeking or accepting exemptions not contemplated in the statutory or regulatory framework related to human rights, environmental, health, safety, labour, taxation, financial incentives, or other issues.
6. Support and uphold good corporate governance principles and develop and apply good corporate governance practices, including throughout enterprise groups.
7. Develop and apply effective self-regulatory practices and management systems that foster a relationship of confidence and mutual trust between enterprises and the societies in which they operate.
8. Promote awareness of and compliance by workers employed by multinational enterprises with respect to company policies through appropriate dissemination of these policies, including through training programmes.

9. Refrain from discriminatory or disciplinary action against workers who make *bona fide* reports to management or, as appropriate, to the competent public authorities, on practices that contravene the law, the *Guidelines* or the enterprise's policies.

10. Carry out risk-based due diligence, for example by incorporating it into their enterprise risk management systems, to identify, prevent and mitigate actual and potential adverse impacts as described in paragraphs 11 and 12, and account for how these impacts are addressed. The nature and extent of due diligence depend on the circumstances of a particular situation.

11. Avoid causing or contributing to adverse impacts on matters covered by the *Guidelines*, through their own activities, and address such impacts when they occur.

12. Seek to prevent or mitigate an adverse impact where they have not contributed to that impact, when the impact is nevertheless directly linked to their operations, products or services by a business relationship. This is not intended to shift responsibility from the entity causing an adverse impact to the enterprise with which it has a business relationship.

13. In addition to addressing adverse impacts in relation to matters covered by the *Guidelines*, encourage, where practicable, business partners, including suppliers and sub-contractors, to apply principles of responsible business conduct compatible with the *Guidelines*.

14. Engage with relevant stakeholders in order to provide meaningful opportunities for their views to be taken into account in relation to planning and decision making for projects or other activities that may significantly impact local communities.

15. Abstain from any improper involvement in local political activities.

B. Enterprises are encouraged to:

1. Support, as appropriate to their circumstances, cooperative efforts in the appropriate fora to promote Internet Freedom through respect of freedom of expression, assembly and association online.

2. Engage in or support, where appropriate, private or multi-stakeholder initiatives and social dialogue on responsible supply chain management while ensuring that these initiatives take due account of their social and economic effects on developing countries and of existing internationally recognised standards.

Commentary on General Policies

1. The General Policies chapter of the *Guidelines* is the first to contain specific recommendations to enterprises. As such it is important for setting the tone and establishing common fundamental principles for the specific recommendations in subsequent chapters.

2. Enterprises are encouraged to co-operate with governments in the development and implementation of policies and laws. Considering the views of other stakeholders in society, which includes the local community as well as business interests, can enrich this process. It is also recognised that governments should be transparent in their dealings with enterprises, and consult with business on these same issues. Enterprises should be viewed as partners with government in the development and use of both voluntary and regulatory approaches (of which the *Guidelines* are one element) to policies affecting them.

3. There should not be any contradiction between the activity of multinational enterprises (MNEs) and sustainable development, and the *Guidelines* are meant to foster complementarities in this regard. Indeed, links among economic, social, and environmental progress are a key means for furthering the goal of sustainable development.[4]

4. Chapter IV elaborates on the general human rights recommendation in paragraph A.2.

5. The *Guidelines* also acknowledge and encourage the contribution that MNEs can make to local capacity building as a result of their activities in local communities. Similarly, the recommendation on human capital formation is an explicit and forward-looking recognition of the contribution to individual human development that MNEs can offer their employees, and encompasses not only hiring practices, but training and other employee development as well. Human capital formation also incorporates the notion of non-discrimination in hiring practices as well as promotion practices, life-long learning and other on-the-job training.

6. The *Guidelines* recommend that, in general, enterprises avoid making efforts to secure exemptions not contemplated in the statutory or regulatory framework related to human rights, environmental, health, safety, labour, taxation and financial incentives among other issues, without infringing on an enterprise's right to seek changes in the

---

4. One of the most broadly accepted definitions of sustainable development is in the 1987 World Commission on Environment and Development (the Brundtland Commission): "Development that meets the needs of the present without compromising the ability of future generations to meet their own needs".

statutory or regulatory framework. The words "or accepting" also draw attention to the role of the State in offering these exemptions. While this sort of provision has been traditionally directed at governments, it is also of direct relevance to MNEs. Importantly, however, there are instances where specific exemptions from laws or other policies can be consistent with these laws for legitimate public policy reasons. The environment and competition policy chapters provide examples.

7. The *Guidelines* recommend that enterprises apply good corporate governance practices drawn from the OECD Principles of Corporate Governance. The Principles call for the protection and facilitation of the exercise of shareholder rights, including the equitable treatment of shareholders. Enterprise should recognise the rights of stakeholders established by law or through mutual agreements and encourage active co-operation with stakeholders in creating wealth, jobs, and the sustainability of financially sound enterprises.

8. The Principles call on the board of the parent entity to ensure the strategic guidance of the enterprise, the effective monitoring of management and to be accountable to the enterprise and to the shareholders, while taking into account the interests of stakeholders. In undertaking these responsibilities, the board needs to ensure the integrity of the enterprise's accounting and financial reporting systems, including independent audit, appropriate control systems, in particular, risk management, and financial and operational control, and compliance with the law and relevant standards.

9. The Principles extend to enterprise groups, although boards of subsidiary enterprises might have obligations under the law of their jurisdiction of incorporation. Compliance and control systems should extend where possible to these subsidiaries. Furthermore, the board's monitoring of governance includes continuous review of internal structures to ensure clear lines of management accountability throughout the group.

10. State-owned multinational enterprises are subject to the same recommendations as privately-owned enterprises, but public scrutiny is often magnified when a State is the final owner. The OECD *Guidelines on Corporate Governance of State-Owned Enterprises* are a useful and specifically tailored guide for these enterprises and the recommendations they offer could significantly improve governance.

11. Although primary responsibility for improving the legal and institutional regulatory framework lies with governments, there is a strong business case for enterprises to implement good corporate governance.

12. An increasing network of non-governmental self-regulatory instruments and actions address aspects of corporate behaviour and the relationships between business and society. Interesting developments in this regard are being undertaken in the financial sector. Enterprises recognise that their activities often have social and environmental implications. The institution of self-regulatory practices and management systems by enterprises sensitive to reaching these goals – thereby contributing to sustainable development – is an illustration of this. In turn, developing such practices can further constructive relationships between enterprises and the societies in which they operate.

13. Following from effective self-regulatory practices, as a matter of course, enterprises are expected to promote employee awareness of company policies. Safeguards to protect bona fide "whistle-blowing" activities are also recommended, including protection of employees who, in the absence of timely remedial action or in the face of reasonable risk of negative employment action, report practices that contravene the law to the competent public authorities. While of particular relevance to anti-bribery and environmental initiatives, such protection is also relevant to other recommendations in the *Guidelines.*

14. For the purposes of the *Guidelines*, due diligence is understood as the process through which enterprises can identify, prevent, mitigate and account for how they address their actual and potential adverse impacts as an integral part of business decision-making and risk management systems. Due diligence can be included within broader enterprise risk management systems, provided that it goes beyond simply identifying and managing material risks to the enterprise itself, to include the risks of adverse impacts related to matters covered by the *Guidelines.* Potential impacts are to be addressed through prevention or mitigation, while actual impacts are to be addressed through remediation. The *Guidelines* concern those adverse impacts that are either caused or contributed to by the enterprise, or are directly linked to their operations, products or services by a business relationship, as described in paragraphs A.11 and A.12. Due diligence can help enterprises avoid the risk of such adverse impacts. For the purposes of this recommendation, 'contributing to' an adverse impact should be interpreted as a substantial contribution, meaning an activity that causes, facilitates or incentivises another entity to cause an adverse impact and does not include minor or trivial contributions. The term 'business relationship' includes relationships with business partners, entities in the supply chain and any other non-State or State entities directly linked to its business operations, products or services. The recommendation in paragraph A.10 applies to those matters covered by the *Guidelines* that are related

to adverse impacts. It does not apply to the chapters on Science and Technology, Competition and Taxation.

15. The nature and extent of due diligence, such as the specific steps to be taken, appropriate to a particular situation will be affected by factors such as the size of the enterprise, context of its operations, the specific recommendations in the *Guidelines*, and the severity of its adverse impacts. Specific recommendations for human rights due diligence are provided in Chapter IV.

16. Where enterprises have large numbers of suppliers, they are encouraged to identify general areas where the risk of adverse impacts is most significant and, based on this risk assessment, prioritise suppliers for due diligence.

17. To avoid causing or contributing to adverse impacts on matters covered by the *Guidelines* through their own activities includes their activities in the supply chain. Relationships in the supply chain take a variety of forms including, for example, franchising, licensing or subcontracting. Entities in the supply chain are often multinational enterprises themselves and, by virtue of this fact, those operating in or from the countries adhering to the Declaration are covered by the *Guidelines*.

18. In the context of its supply chain, if the enterprise identifies a risk of causing an adverse impact, then it should take the necessary steps to cease or prevent that impact.

19. If the enterprise identifies a risk of contributing to an adverse impact, then it should take the necessary steps to cease or prevent its contribution and use its leverage to mitigate any remaining impacts to the greatest extent possible. Leverage is considered to exist where the enterprise has the ability to effect change in the wrongful practices of the entity that causes the harm.

20. Meeting the expectation in paragraph A.12 would entail an enterprise, acting alone or in co-operation with other entities, as appropriate, to use its leverage to influence the entity causing the adverse impact to prevent or mitigate that impact.

21. The *Guidelines* recognise that there are practical limitations on the ability of enterprises to effect change in the behaviour of their suppliers. These are related to product characteristics, the number of suppliers, the structure and complexity of the supply chain, the market position of the enterprise vis-à-vis its suppliers or other entities in the supply chain. However, enterprises can also influence suppliers through contractual arrangements such as management contracts, pre-qualification requirements for potential suppliers, voting trusts, and licence or

franchise agreements. Other factors relevant to determining the appropriate response to the identified risks include the severity and probability of adverse impacts and how crucial that supplier is to the enterprise.

22. Appropriate responses with regard to the business relationship may include continuation of the relationship with a supplier throughout the course of risk mitigation efforts; temporary suspension of the relationship while pursuing ongoing risk mitigation; or, as a last resort, disengagement with the supplier either after failed attempts at mitigation, or where the enterprise deems mitigation not feasible, or because of the severity of the adverse impact. The enterprise should also take into account potential social and economic adverse impacts related to the decision to disengage.

23. Enterprises may also engage with suppliers and other entities in the supply chain to improve their performance, in co-operation with other stakeholders, including through personnel training and other forms of capacity building, and to support the integration of principles of responsible business conduct compatible with the *Guidelines* into their business practices. Where suppliers have multiple customers and are potentially exposed to conflicting requirements imposed by different buyers, enterprises are encouraged, with due regard to anti-competitive concerns, to participate in industry-wide collaborative efforts with other enterprises with which they share common suppliers to coordinate supply chain policies and risk management strategies, including through information-sharing.

24. Enterprises are also encouraged to participate in private or multi-stakeholder initiatives and social dialogue on responsible supply chain management, such as those undertaken as part of the proactive agenda pursuant to the Decision of the OECD Council on the OECD *Guidelines for Multinational Enterprises* and the attached Procedural Guidance.

25. Stakeholder engagement involves interactive processes of engagement with relevant stakeholders, through, for example, meetings, hearings or consultation proceedings. Effective stakeholder engagement is characterised by two-way communication and depends on the good faith of the participants on both sides. This engagement can be particularly helpful in the planning and decision-making concerning projects or other activities involving, for example, the intensive use of land or water, which could significantly affect local communities.

26. Paragraph B.1 acknowledges an important emerging issue. It does not create new standards, nor does it presume the development of new standards. It recognises that enterprises have interests which will be

affected and that their participation along with other stakeholders in discussion of the issues involved can contribute to their ability and that of others to understand the issues and make a positive contribution. It recognises that the issues may have a number of dimensions and emphasises that co-operation should be pursued through appropriate fora. It is without prejudice to positions held by governments in the area of electronic commerce at the World Trade Organisation (WTO). It is not intended to disregard other important public policy interests which may relate to the use of the internet which would need to be taken into account.[5] Finally, as is the case with the *Guidelines* in general, it is not intended to create conflicting requirements for enterprises consistent with paragraphs 2 and 8 of the Concepts and Principles Chapter of the *Guidelines*.

27. Finally, it is important to note that self-regulation and other initiatives in a similar vein, including the *Guidelines*, should not unlawfully restrict competition, nor should they be considered a substitute for effective law and regulation by governments. It is understood that MNEs should avoid potential trade or investment distorting effects of codes and self-regulatory practices when they are being developed.

5. Some countries have referred to the 2005 Tunis Agenda for the Information Society in this regard.

III. Disclosure

1. Enterprises should ensure that timely and accurate information is disclosed on all material matters regarding their activities, structure, financial situation, performance, ownership and governance. This information should be disclosed for the enterprise as a whole, and, where appropriate, along business lines or geographic areas. Disclosure policies of enterprises should be tailored to the nature, size and location of the enterprise, with due regard taken of costs, business confidentiality and other competitive concerns.

2. Disclosure policies of enterprises should include, but not be limited to, material information on:

   a) the financial and operating results of the enterprise;

   b) enterprise objectives;

   c) major share ownership and voting rights, including the structure of a group of enterprises and intra-group relations, as well as control enhancing mechanisms;

   d) remuneration policy for members of the board and key executives, and information about board members, including qualifications, the selection process, other enterprise directorships and whether each board member is regarded as independent by the board;

   e) related party transactions;

   f) foreseeable risk factors;

   g) issues regarding workers and other stakeholders;

   h) governance structures and policies, in particular, the content of any corporate governance code or policy and its implementation process.

3. Enterprises are encouraged to communicate additional information that could include:

   a) value statements or statements of business conduct intended for public disclosure including, depending on its relevance for the enterprise's activities, information on the enterprise's policies relating to matters covered by the *Guidelines*;

b) policies and other codes of conduct to which the enterprise subscribes, their date of adoption and the countries and entities to which such statements apply;

c) its performance in relation to these statements and codes;

d) information on internal audit, risk management and legal compliance systems;

e) information on relationships with workers and other stakeholders.

4. Enterprises should apply high quality standards for accounting, and financial as well as non-financial disclosure, including environmental and social reporting where they exist. The standards or policies under which information is compiled and published should be reported. An annual audit should be conducted by an independent, competent and qualified auditor in order to provide an external and objective assurance to the board and shareholders that the financial statements fairly represent the financial position and performance of the enterprise in all material respects.

Commentary on Disclosure

28. The purpose of this chapter is to encourage improved understanding of the operations of multinational enterprises. Clear and complete information on enterprises is important to a variety of users ranging from shareholders and the financial community to other constituencies such as workers, local communities, special interest groups, governments and society at large. To improve public understanding of enterprises and their interaction with society and the environment, enterprises should be transparent in their operations and responsive to the public's increasingly sophisticated demands for information.

29. The information highlighted in this chapter addresses disclosure in two areas. The first set of disclosure recommendations is identical to disclosure items outlined in the OECD Principles of Corporate Governance. Their related annotations provide further guidance and the recommendations in the *Guidelines* should be construed in relation to them. The first set of disclosure recommendations may be supplemented by a second set of disclosure recommendations which enterprises are encouraged to follow. The disclosure recommendations focus mainly on publicly traded enterprises. To the extent that they are deemed applicable in light of the nature, size and location of enterprises, they

should also be a useful tool to improve corporate governance in non-traded enterprises; for example, privately held or State-owned enterprises.

30. Disclosure recommendations are not expected to place unreasonable administrative or cost burdens on enterprises. Nor are enterprises expected to disclose information that may endanger their competitive position unless disclosure is necessary to fully inform the investment decision and to avoid misleading the investor. In order to determine what information should be disclosed at a minimum, the *Guidelines* use the concept of materiality. Material information can be defined as information whose omission or misstatement could influence the economic decisions taken by users of information.

31. The *Guidelines* also generally note that information should be prepared and disclosed in accordance with high quality standards of accounting and financial and non-financial disclosure. This significantly improves the ability of investors to monitor the enterprise by providing increased reliability and comparability of reporting, and improved insight into its performance. The annual independent audit recommended by the *Guidelines* should contribute to an improved control and compliance by the enterprise.

32. Disclosure is addressed in two areas. The first set of disclosure recommendations calls for timely and accurate disclosure on all material matters regarding the corporation, including the financial situation, performance, ownership and governance of the company. Companies are also expected to disclose sufficient information on the remuneration of board members and key executives (either individually or in the aggregate) for investors to properly assess the costs and benefits of remuneration plans and the contribution of incentive schemes, such as stock option schemes, to performance. Related party transactions and material foreseeable risk factors are additional relevant information that should be disclosed, as well as material issues regarding workers and other stakeholders.

33. The *Guidelines* also encourage a second set of disclosure or communication practices in areas where reporting standards are still evolving such as, for example, social, environmental and risk reporting. This is particularly the case with greenhouse gas emissions, as the scope of their monitoring is expanding to cover direct and indirect, current and future, corporate and product emissions; biodiversity is another example. Many enterprises provide information on a broader set of topics than financial performance and consider disclosure of such information a method by which they can demonstrate a commitment to

socially acceptable practices. In some cases, this second type of disclosure – or communication with the public and with other parties directly affected by the enterprise's activities – may pertain to entities that extend beyond those covered in the enterprise's financial accounts. For example, it may also cover information on the activities of subcontractors and suppliers or of joint venture partners. This is particularly appropriate to monitor the transfer of environmentally harmful activities to partners.

34. Many enterprises have adopted measures designed to help them comply with the law and standards of business conduct, and to enhance the transparency of their operations. A growing number of firms have issued voluntary codes of corporate conduct, which are expressions of commitments to ethical values in such areas as environment, human rights, labour standards, consumer protection, or taxation. Specialised management systems have been or are being developed and continue to evolve with the aim of helping them respect these commitments – these involve information systems, operating procedures and training requirements. Enterprises are cooperating with NGOs and intergovernmental organisations in developing reporting standards that enhance enterprises' ability to communicate how their activities influence sustainable development outcomes (for example, the Global Reporting Initiative).

35. Enterprises are encouraged to provide easy and economical access to published information and to consider making use of information technologies to meet this goal. Information that is made available to users in home markets should also be available to all interested users. Enterprises may take special steps to make information available to communities that do not have access to printed media (for example, poorer communities that are directly affected by the enterprise's activities).

IV. Human Rights

States have the duty to protect human rights. Enterprises should, within the framework of internationally recognised human rights, the international human rights obligations of the countries in which they operate as well as relevant domestic laws and regulations:

1. Respect human rights, which means they should avoid infringing on the human rights of others and should address adverse human rights impacts with which they are involved.
2. Within the context of their own activities, avoid causing or contributing to adverse human rights impacts and address such impacts when they occur.
3. Seek ways to prevent or mitigate adverse human rights impacts that are directly linked to their business operations, products or services by a business relationship, even if they do not contribute to those impacts.
4. Have a policy commitment to respect human rights.
5. Carry out human rights due diligence as appropriate to their size, the nature and context of operations and the severity of the risks of adverse human rights impacts.
6. Provide for or co-operate through legitimate processes in the remediation of adverse human rights impacts where they identify that they have caused or contributed to these impacts.

Commentary on Human Rights

36. This chapter opens with a chapeau that sets out the framework for the specific recommendations concerning enterprises' respect for human rights. It draws upon the United Nations Framework for Business and Human Rights 'Protect, Respect and Remedy' and is in line with the Guiding Principles for its Implementation.
37. The chapeau and the first paragraph recognise that States have the duty to protect human rights, and that enterprises, regardless of their size,

sector, operational context, ownership and structure, should respect human rights wherever they operate. Respect for human rights is the global standard of expected conduct for enterprises independently of States' abilities and/or willingness to fulfil their human rights obligations, and does not diminish those obligations.

38. A State's failure either to enforce relevant domestic laws, or to implement international human rights obligations or the fact that it may act contrary to such laws or international obligations does not diminish the expectation that enterprises respect human rights. In countries where domestic laws and regulations conflict with internationally recognised human rights, enterprises should seek ways to honour them to the fullest extent which does not place them in violation of domestic law, consistent with paragraph 2 of the Chapter on Concepts and Principles.

39. In all cases and irrespective of the country or specific context of enterprises' operations, reference should be made at a minimum to the internationally recognised human rights expressed in the International Bill of Human Rights, consisting of the Universal Declaration of Human Rights and the main instruments through which it has been codified: the International Covenant on Civil and Political Rights and the International Covenant on Economic, Social and Cultural Rights, and to the principles concerning fundamental rights set out in the 1998 International Labour Organisation Declaration on Fundamental Principles and Rights at Work.

40. Enterprises can have an impact on virtually the entire spectrum of internationally recognised human rights. In practice, some human rights may be at greater risk than others in particular industries or contexts, and therefore will be the focus of heightened attention. However, situations may change, so all rights should be the subject of periodic review. Depending on circumstances, enterprises may need to consider additional standards. For instance, enterprises should respect the human rights of individuals belonging to specific groups or populations that require particular attention, where they may have adverse human rights impacts on them. In this connection, United Nations instruments have elaborated further on the rights of indigenous peoples; persons belonging to national or ethnic, religious and linguistic minorities; women; children; persons with disabilities; and migrant workers and their families. Moreover, in situations of armed conflict enterprises should respect the standards of international humanitarian law, which can help enterprises avoid the risks of causing or contributing to adverse impacts when operating in such difficult environments.

41. In paragraph 1, addressing actual and potential adverse human rights impacts consists of taking adequate measures for their identification, prevention, where possible, and mitigation of potential human rights impacts, remediation of actual impacts, and accounting for how the adverse human rights impacts are addressed. The term 'infringing' refers to adverse impacts that an enterprise may have on the human rights of individuals.

42. Paragraph 2 recommends that enterprises avoid causing or contributing to adverse human rights impacts through their own activities and address such impacts when they occur. 'Activities' can include both actions and omissions. Where an enterprise causes or may cause an adverse human rights impact, it should take the necessary steps to cease or prevent the impact. Where an enterprise contributes or may contribute to such an impact, it should take the necessary steps to cease or prevent its contribution and use its leverage to mitigate any remaining impact to the greatest extent possible. Leverage is considered to exist where the enterprise has the ability to effect change in the practices of an entity that cause adverse human rights impacts.

43. Paragraph 3 addresses more complex situations where an enterprise has not contributed to an adverse human rights impact, but that impact is nevertheless directly linked to its operations, products or services by its business relationship with another entity. Paragraph 3 is not intended to shift responsibility from the entity causing an adverse human rights impact to the enterprise with which it has a business relationship. Meeting the expectation in paragraph 3 would entail an enterprise, acting alone or in co-operation with other entities, as appropriate, to use its leverage to influence the entity causing the adverse human rights impact to prevent or mitigate that impact. 'Business relationships' include relationships with business partners, entities in its supply chain, and any other non-State or State entity directly linked to its business operations, products or services. Among the factors that will enter into the determination of the appropriate action in such situations are the enterprise's leverage over the entity concerned, how crucial the relationship is to the enterprise, the severity of the impact, and whether terminating the relationship with the entity itself would have adverse human rights impacts.

44. Paragraph 4 recommends that enterprises express their commitment to respect human rights through a statement of policy that: *(i)* is approved at the most senior level of the enterprise; *(ii)* is informed by relevant internal and/or external expertise; *(iii)* stipulates the enterprise's human rights expectations of personnel, business partners and other parties directly linked to its operations, products or services; *(iv)* is publicly

available and communicated internally and externally to all personnel, business partners and other relevant parties; *(v)* is reflected in operational policies and procedures necessary to embed it throughout the enterprise.

45. Paragraph 5 recommends that enterprises carry out human rights due diligence. The process entails assessing actual and potential human rights impacts, integrating and acting upon the findings, tracking responses as well as communicating how impacts are addressed. Human rights due diligence can be included within broader enterprise risk management systems provided that it goes beyond simply identifying and managing material risks to the enterprise itself to include the risks to rights-holders. It is an on-going exercise, recognising that human rights risks may change over time as the enterprise's operations and operating context evolve. Complementary guidance on due diligence, including in relation to supply chains, and appropriate responses to risks arising in supply chains are provided under paragraphs A.10 to A.12 of the Chapter on General Policies and their Commentaries.

46. When enterprises identify through their human rights due diligence process or other means that they have caused or contributed to an adverse impact, the *Guidelines* recommend that enterprises have processes in place to enable remediation. Some situations require co-operation with judicial or State-based non-judicial mechanisms. In others, operational-level grievance mechanisms for those potentially impacted by enterprises' activities can be an effective means of providing for such processes when they meet the core criteria of: legitimacy, accessibility, predictability, equitability, compatibility with the *Guidelines* and transparency, and are based on dialogue and engagement with a view to seeking agreed solutions. Such mechanisms can be administered by an enterprise alone or in collaboration with other stakeholders and can be a source of continuous learning. Operational-level grievance mechanisms should not be used to undermine the role of trade unions in addressing labour-related disputes, nor should such mechanisms preclude access to judicial or non-judicial grievance mechanisms, including the National Contact Points under the *Guidelines*.

V. Employment and Industrial Relations

Enterprises should, within the framework of applicable law, regulations and prevailing labour relations and employment practices and applicable international labour standards:

1. a) Respect the right of workers employed by the multinational enterprise to establish or join trade unions and representative organisations of their own choosing.

   b) Respect the right of workers employed by the multinational enterprise to have trade unions and representative organisations of their own choosing recognised for the purpose of collective bargaining, and engage in constructive negotiations, either individually or through employers' associations, with such representatives with a view to reaching agreements on terms and conditions of employment.

   c) Contribute to the effective abolition of child labour, and take immediate and effective measures to secure the prohibition and elimination of the worst forms of child labour as a matter of urgency.

   d) Contribute to the elimination of all forms of forced or compulsory labour and take adequate steps to ensure that forced or compulsory labour does not exist in their operations.

   e) Be guided throughout their operations by the principle of equality of opportunity and treatment in employment and not discriminate against their workers with respect to employment or occupation on such grounds as race, colour, sex, religion, political opinion, national extraction or social origin, or other status, unless selectivity concerning worker characteristics furthers established governmental policies which specifically promote greater equality of employment opportunity or relates to the inherent requirements of a job.

2. a) Provide such facilities to workers' representatives as may be necessary to assist in the development of effective collective agreements.

b) Provide information to workers' representatives which is needed for meaningful negotiations on conditions of employment.

c) Provide information to workers and their representatives which enables them to obtain a true and fair view of the performance of the entity or, where appropriate, the enterprise as a whole.

3. Promote consultation and co-operation between employers and workers and their representatives on matters of mutual concern.

4. a) Observe standards of employment and industrial relations not less favourable than those observed by comparable employers in the host country.

b) When multinational enterprises operate in developing countries, where comparable employers may not exist, provide the best possible wages, benefits and conditions of work, within the framework of government policies. These should be related to the economic position of the enterprise, but should be at least adequate to satisfy the basic needs of the workers and their families.

c) Take adequate steps to ensure occupational health and safety in their operations.

5. In their operations, to the greatest extent practicable, employ local workers and provide training with a view to improving skill levels, in co-operation with worker representatives and, where appropriate, relevant governmental authorities.

6. In considering changes in their operations which would have major employment effects, in particular in the case of the closure of an entity involving collective lay-offs or dismissals, provide reasonable notice of such changes to representatives of the workers in their employment and their organisations, and, where appropriate, to the relevant governmental authorities, and co-operate with the worker representatives and appropriate governmental authorities so as to mitigate to the maximum extent practicable adverse effects. In light of the specific circumstances of each case, it would be appropriate if management were able to give such notice prior to the final decision being taken. Other means may also be employed to provide meaningful co-operation to mitigate the effects of such decisions.

7. In the context of bona fide negotiations with workers' representatives on conditions of employment, or while workers are exercising a right to organise, not threaten to transfer the whole or part of an operating unit from the country concerned nor transfer workers from the enterprises'

component entities in other countries in order to influence unfairly those negotiations or to hinder the exercise of a right to organise.

8. Enable authorised representatives of the workers in their employment to negotiate on collective bargaining or labour-management relations issues and allow the parties to consult on matters of mutual concern with representatives of management who are authorised to take decisions on these matters.

Commentary on Employment and Industrial Relations

47. This chapter opens with a chapeau that includes a reference to "applicable" law and regulations, which is meant to acknowledge the fact that multinational enterprises, while operating within the jurisdiction of particular countries, may be subject to national and international levels of regulation of employment and industrial relations matters. The terms "prevailing labour relations" and "employment practices" are sufficiently broad to permit a variety of interpretations in light of different national circumstances – for example, different bargaining options provided for workers under national laws and regulations.

48. The International Labour Organisation (ILO) is the competent body to set and deal with international labour standards, and to promote fundamental rights at work as recognised in its 1998 Declaration on Fundamental Principles and Rights at Work. The *Guidelines*, as a non-binding instrument, have a role to play in promoting observance of these standards and principles among multinational enterprises. The provisions of the *Guidelines* chapter echo relevant provisions of the 1998 Declaration, as well as the 1977 ILO Tripartite Declaration of Principles concerning Multinational Enterprises and Social Policy, last revised in 2006 (the ILO MNE Declaration). The ILO MNE Declaration sets out principles in the fields of employment, training, working conditions, and industrial relations, while the OECD *Guidelines* cover all major aspects of corporate behaviour. The OECD *Guidelines* and the ILO MNE Declaration refer to the behaviour expected from enterprises and are intended to parallel and not conflict with each other. The ILO MNE Declaration can therefore be of use in understanding the *Guidelines* to the extent that it is of a greater degree of elaboration. However, the responsibilities for the follow-up procedures under the ILO MNE Declaration and the *Guidelines* are institutionally separate.

49. The terminology used in Chapter V is consistent with that used in the ILO MNE Declaration. The use of the terms "workers employed by the

multinational enterprise" and "workers in their employment" is intended to have the same meaning as in the ILO MNE Declaration. These terms refer to workers who are "in an employment relationship with the multinational enterprise". Enterprises wishing to understand the scope of their responsibility under Chapter V will find useful guidance for determining the existence of an employment relationship in the context of the *Guidelines* in the non-exhaustive list of indicators set forth in ILO Recommendation 198 of 2006, paragraphs 13 (a) and (b). In addition, it is recognised that working arrangements change and develop over time and that enterprises are expected to structure their relationships with workers so as to avoid supporting, encouraging or participating in disguised employment practices. A disguised employment relationship occurs when an employer treats an individual as other than an employee in a manner that hides his or her true legal status.

50. These recommendations do not interfere with true civil and commercial relationships, but rather seek to ensure that individuals in an employment relationship have the protection that is due to them in the context of the *Guidelines*. It is recognised that in the absence of an employment relationship, enterprises are nevertheless expected to act in accordance with the risk-based due diligence and supply chain recommendations in paragraphs A.10 to A.13 of Chapter II on General Policies.

51. Paragraph 1 of this chapter is designed to echo all four fundamental principles and rights at work which are contained in the ILO's 1998 Declaration, namely the freedom of association and right to collective bargaining, the effective abolition of child labour, the elimination of all forms of forced or compulsory labour, and non-discrimination in employment and occupation. These principles and rights have been developed in the form of specific rights and obligations in ILO Conventions recognised as fundamental.

52. Paragraph 1c) recommends that multinational enterprises contribute to the effective abolition of child labour in the sense of the ILO 1998 Declaration and ILO Convention 182 concerning the worst forms of child labour. Long-standing ILO instruments on child labour are Convention 138 and Recommendation 146 (both adopted in 1973) concerning minimum ages for employment. Through their labour management practices, their creation of high-quality, well-paid jobs and their contribution to economic growth, multinational enterprises can play a positive role in helping to address the root causes of poverty in general and of child labour in particular. It is important to acknowledge and encourage the role of multinational enterprises in contributing to the search for a lasting solution to the problem of child labour. In this

regard, raising the standards of education of children living in host countries is especially noteworthy.

53. Paragraph 1d) recommends that enterprises contribute to the elimination of all forms of forced and compulsory labour, another principle derived from the 1998 ILO Declaration. The reference to this core labour right is based on the ILO Conventions 29 of 1930 and 105 of 1957. Convention 29 requests that governments "suppress the use of forced or compulsory labour in all its forms within the shortest possible period", while Convention 105 requests of them to "suppress and not to make use of any form of forced or compulsory labour" for certain enumerated purposes (for example, as a means of political coercion or labour discipline), and "to take effective measures to secure [its] immediate and complete abolition". At the same time, it is understood that the ILO is the competent body to deal with the difficult issue of prison labour, in particular when it comes to the hiring-out of prisoners to (or their placing at the disposal of) private individuals, companics or associations.

54. The reference to the principle of non-discrimination with respect to employment and occupation in paragraph 1e is considered to apply to such terms and conditions as hiring, job assignment, discharge, pay and benefits, promotion, transfer or relocation, termination, training and retirement. The list of non-permissible grounds for discrimination which is taken from ILO Convention 111 of 1958, the Maternity Protection Convention 183 of 2000, Employment (Disabled Persons) Convention 159 of 1983, the Older Workers Recommendation 162 of 1980 and the HIV and AIDS at Work Recommendation 200 of 2010, considers that any distinction, exclusion or preference on these grounds is in violation of the Conventions, Recommendations and Codes. The term "other status" for the purposes of the *Guidelines* refers to trade union activity and personal characteristics such as age, disability, pregnancy, marital status, sexual orientation, or HIV status. Consistent with the provisions in paragraph 1e, enterprises are expected to promote equal opportunities for women and men with special emphasis on equal criteria for selection, remuneration, and promotion, and equal application of those criteria, and prevent discrimination or dismissals on the grounds of marriage, pregnancy or parenthood.

55. In paragraph 2c) of this chapter, information provided by companies to their workers and their representatives is expected to provide a "true and fair view" of performance. It relates to the following: the structure of the enterprise, its economic and financial situation and prospects, employment trends, and expected substantial changes in operations, taking into account legitimate requirements of business confidentiality.

Considerations of business confidentiality may mean that information on certain points may not be provided, or may not be provided without safeguards.

56. The reference to consultative forms of worker participation in paragraph 3 of the Chapter is taken from ILO Recommendation 94 of 1952 concerning Consultation and Co-operation between Employers and Workers at the Level of the Undertaking. It also conforms to a provision contained in the ILO MNE Declaration. Such consultative arrangements should not substitute for workers' right to bargain over terms and conditions of employment. A recommendation on consultative arrangements with respect to working arrangements is also part of paragraph 8.

57. In paragraph 4, employment and industrial relations standards are understood to include compensation and working-time arrangements. The reference to occupational health and safety implies that multinational enterprises are expected to follow prevailing regulatory standards and industry norms to minimise the risk of accidents and injury to health arising out of, linked with, or occurring in, the course of employment. This encourages enterprises to work to raise the level of performance with respect to occupational health and safety in all parts of their operation even where this may not be formally required by existing regulations in countries in which they operate. It also encourages enterprises to respect workers' ability to remove themselves from a work situation when there is reasonable justification to believe that it presents an imminent and serious risk to health or safety. Reflecting their importance and complementarities among related recommendations, health and safety concerns are echoed elsewhere in the *Guidelines*, most notably in chapters on Consumer Interests and the Environment. The ILO Recommendation No. 194 of 2002 provides an indicative list of occupational diseases as well as codes of practice and guides which can be taken into account by enterprises for implementing this recommendation of the *Guidelines*.

58. The recommendation in paragraph 5 of the chapter encourages MNEs to recruit an adequate workforce share locally, including managerial personnel, and to provide training to them. Language in this paragraph on training and skill levels complements the text in paragraph A.4 of the General Policies chapter on encouraging human capital formation. The reference to local workers complements the text encouraging local capacity building in paragraph A.3 of the General Policies chapter. In accordance with the ILO Human Resources Development Recommendation 195 of 2004, enterprises are also encouraged to invest, to the greatest extent practicable, in training and lifelong learning while

ensuring equal opportunities to training for women and other vulnerable groups, such as youth, low-skilled people, people with disabilities, migrants, older workers, and indigenous peoples.

59. Paragraph 6 recommends that enterprises provide reasonable notice to the representatives of workers and relevant government authorities, of changes in their operations which would have major effects upon the livelihood of their workers, in particular the closure of an entity involving collective layoffs or dismissals. As stated therein, the purpose of this provision is to afford an opportunity for co-operation to mitigate the effects of such changes. This is an important principle that is widely reflected in the industrial relations laws and practices of adhering countries, although the approaches taken to ensuring an opportunity for meaningful co-operation are not identical in all adhering countries. The paragraph also notes that it would be appropriate if, in light of specific circumstances, management were able to give such notice prior to the final decision. Indeed, notice prior to the final decision is a feature of industrial relations laws and practices in a number of adhering countries. However, it is not the only means to ensure an opportunity for meaningful co-operation to mitigate the effects of such decisions, and the laws and practices of other adhering countries provide for other means such as defined periods during which consultations must be undertaken before decisions may be implemented.

VI. Environment

Enterprises should, within the framework of laws, regulations and administrative practices in the countries in which they operate, and in consideration of relevant international agreements, principles, objectives, and standards, take due account of the need to protect the environment, public health and safety, and generally to conduct their activities in a manner contributing to the wider goal of sustainable development. In particular, enterprises should:

1. Establish and maintain a system of environmental management appropriate to the enterprise, including:

   a) collection and evaluation of adequate and timely information regarding the environmental, health, and safety impacts of their activities;

   b) establishment of measurable objectives and, where appropriate, targets for improved environmental performance and resource utilisation, including periodically reviewing the continuing relevance of these objectives; where appropriate, targets should be consistent with relevant national policies and international environmental commitments; and

   c) regular monitoring and verification of progress toward environmental, health, and safety objectives or targets.

2. Taking into account concerns about cost, business confidentiality, and the protection of intellectual property rights:

   a) provide the public and workers with adequate, measureable and verifiable (where applicable) and timely information on the potential environment, health and safety impacts of the activities of the enterprise, which could include reporting on progress in improving environmental performance; and

   b) engage in adequate and timely communication and consultation with the communities directly affected by the environmental, health and safety policies of the enterprise and by their implementation.

3. Assess, and address in decision-making, the foreseeable environmental, health, and safety-related impacts associated with the processes, goods and services of the enterprise over their full life cycle with a view to avoiding or, when unavoidable, mitigating them. Where these proposed activities may have significant environmental, health, or safety impacts, and where they are subject to a decision of a competent authority, prepare an appropriate environmental impact assessment.

4. Consistent with the scientific and technical understanding of the risks, where there are threats of serious damage to the environment, taking also into account human health and safety, not use the lack of full scientific certainty as a reason for postponing cost-effective measures to prevent or minimise such damage.

5. Maintain contingency plans for preventing, mitigating, and controlling serious environmental and health damage from their operations, including accidents and emergencies; and mechanisms for immediate reporting to the competent authorities.

6. Continually seek to improve corporate environmental performance, at the level of the enterprise and, where appropriate, of its supply chain, by encouraging such activities as:

   a) adoption of technologies and operating procedures in all parts of the enterprise that reflect standards concerning environmental performance in the best performing part of the enterprise;

   b) development and provision of products or services that have no undue environmental impacts; are safe in their intended use; reduce greenhouse gas emissions; are efficient in their consumption of energy and natural resources; can be reused, recycled, or disposed of safely;

   c) promoting higher levels of awareness among customers of the environmental implications of using the products and services of the enterprise, including, by providing accurate information on their products (for example, on greenhouse gas emissions, biodiversity, resource efficiency, or other environmental issues); and

   d) exploring and assessing ways of improving the environmental performance of the enterprise over the longer term, for instance by developing strategies for emission reduction, efficient resource utilisation and recycling, substitution or reduction of use of toxic substances, or strategies on biodiversity.

7. Provide adequate education and training to workers in environmental health and safety matters, including the handling of hazardous materials and the prevention of environmental accidents, as well as more general environmental management areas, such as environmental impact assessment procedures, public relations, and environmental technologies.

8. Contribute to the development of environmentally meaningful and economically efficient public policy, for example, by means of partnerships or initiatives that will enhance environmental awareness and protection.

Commentary on the Environment

60. The text of the Environment Chapter broadly reflects the principles and objectives contained in the Rio Declaration on Environment and Development, in Agenda 21 (within the Rio Declaration). It also takes into account the (Aarhus) Convention on Access to Information, Public Participation in Decision-making, and Access to Justice in Environmental Matters and reflects standards contained in such instruments as the ISO Standard on Environmental Management Systems.

61. Sound environmental management is an important part of sustainable development, and is increasingly being seen as both a business responsibility and a business opportunity. Multinational enterprises have a role to play in both respects. Managers of these enterprises should therefore give appropriate attention to environmental issues within their business strategies. Improving environmental performance requires a commitment to a systematic approach and to continual improvement of the system. An environmental management system provides the internal framework necessary to control an enterprise's environmental impacts and to integrate environmental considerations into business operations. Having such a system in place should help to assure shareholders, employees and the community that the enterprise is actively working to protect the environment from the impacts of its activities.

62. In addition to improving environmental performance, instituting an environmental management system can provide economic benefits to companies through reduced operating and insurance costs, improved energy and resource conservation, reduced compliance and liability charges, improved access to capital and skills, improved customer satisfaction, and improved community and public relations.

63. In the context of these *Guidelines*, "sound environmental management" should be interpreted in its broadest sense, embodying activities aimed at controlling both direct and indirect environmental impacts of enterprise activities over the long-term, and involving both pollution control and resource management elements.

64. In most enterprises, an internal control system is needed to manage the enterprise's activities. The environmental part of this system may include such elements as targets for improved performance and regular monitoring of progress towards these targets.

65. Information about the activities of enterprises and about their relationships with sub-contractors and their suppliers, and associated environmental impacts is an important vehicle for building confidence with the public. This vehicle is most effective when information is provided in a transparent manner and when it encourages active consultation with stakeholders such as employees, customers, suppliers, contractors, local communities and with the public-at-large so as to promote a climate of long-term trust and understanding on environmental issues of mutual interest. Reporting and communication are particularly appropriate where scarce or at risk environmental assets are at stake either in a regional, national or international context; reporting standards such as the Global Reporting Initiative provide useful references.

66. In providing accurate information on their products, enterprises have several options such as voluntary labelling or certification schemes. In using these instruments enterprises should take due account of their social and economic effects on developing countries and of existing internationally recognised standards.

67. Normal business activity can involve the *ex ante* assessment of the potential environmental impacts associated with the enterprise's activities. Enterprises often carry out appropriate environmental impact assessments, even if they are not required by law. Environmental assessments made by the enterprise may contain a broad and forward-looking view of the potential impacts of an enterprise's activities and of activities of sub-contractors and suppliers, addressing relevant impacts and examining alternatives and mitigation measures to avoid or redress adverse impacts. The *Guidelines* also recognise that multinational enterprises have certain responsibilities in other parts of the product life cycle.

68. Several instruments already adopted by countries adhering to the *Guidelines*, including Principle 15 of the Rio Declaration on Environment and Development, enunciate a "precautionary approach".

None of these instruments is explicitly addressed to enterprises, although enterprise contributions are implicit in all of them.

69. The basic premise of the *Guidelines* is that enterprises should act as soon as possible, and in a proactive way, to avoid, for instance, serious or irreversible environmental damages resulting from their activities. However, the fact that the *Guidelines* are addressed to enterprises means that no existing instrument is completely adequate for expressing this recommendation. The *Guidelines* therefore draw upon, but do not completely mirror, any existing instrument.

70. The *Guidelines* are not intended to reinterpret any existing instruments or to create new commitments or precedents on the part of governments – they are intended only to recommend how the precautionary approach should be implemented at the level of enterprises. Given the early stage of this process, it is recognised that some flexibility is needed in its application, based on the specific context in which it is carried out. It is also recognised that governments determine the basic framework in this field, and have the responsibility to consult periodically with stakeholders on the most appropriate ways forward.

71. The *Guidelines* also encourage enterprises to work to raise the level of environmental performance in all parts of their operations, even where this may not be formally required by existing practice in the countries in which they operate. In this regard, enterprises should take due account of their social and economic effects on developing countries.

72. For example, multinational enterprises often have access to existing and innovative technologies or operating procedures which could, if applied, help raise environmental performance overall. Multinational enterprises are frequently regarded as leaders in their respective fields, so the potential for a "demonstration effect" on other enterprises should not be overlooked. Ensuring that the environment of the countries in which multinational enterprises operate also benefit from available and innovative technologies and practices, is an important way of building support for international investment activities more generally.

73. Enterprises have an important role to play in the training and education of their employees with regard to environmental matters. They are encouraged to discharge this responsibility in as broad a manner as possible, especially in areas directly related to human health and safety.

VII. Combating Bribery, Bribe Solicitation and Extortion

Enterprises should not, directly or indirectly, offer, promise, give, or demand a bribe or other undue advantage to obtain or retain business or other improper advantage. Enterprises should also resist the solicitation of bribes and extortion. In particular, enterprises should:

1. Not offer, promise or give undue pecuniary or other advantage to public officials or the employees of business partners. Likewise, enterprises should not request, agree to or accept undue pecuniary or other advantage from public officials or the employees of business partners. Enterprises should not use third parties such as agents and other intermediaries, consultants, representatives, distributors, consortia, contractors and suppliers and joint venture partners for channelling undue pecuniary or other advantages to public officials, or to employees of their business partners or to their relatives or business associates.

2. Develop and adopt adequate internal controls, ethics and compliance programmes or measures for preventing and detecting bribery, developed on the basis of a risk assessment addressing the individual circumstances of an enterprise, in particular the bribery risks facing the enterprise (such as its geographical and industrial sector of operation). These internal controls, ethics and compliance programmes or measures should include a system of financial and accounting procedures, including a system of internal controls, reasonably designed to ensure the maintenance of fair and accurate books, records, and accounts, to ensure that they cannot be used for the purpose of bribing or hiding bribery. Such individual circumstances and bribery risks should be regularly monitored and re-assessed as necessary to ensure the enterprise's internal controls, ethics and compliance programme or measures are adapted and continue to be effective, and to mitigate the risk of enterprises becoming complicit in bribery, bribe solicitation and extortion.

3. Prohibit or discourage, in internal company controls, ethics and compliance programmes or measures, the use of small facilitation

payments, which are generally illegal in the countries where they are made, and, when such payments are made, accurately record these in books and financial records.

4. Ensure, taking into account the particular bribery risks facing the enterprise, properly documented due diligence pertaining to the hiring, as well as the appropriate and regular oversight of agents, and that remuneration of agents is appropriate and for legitimate services only. Where relevant, a list of agents engaged in connection with transactions with public bodies and State-owned enterprises should be kept and made available to competent authorities, in accordance with applicable public disclosure requirements.

5. Enhance the transparency of their activities in the fight against bribery, bribe solicitation and extortion. Measures could include making public commitments against bribery, bribe solicitation and extortion, and disclosing the management systems and the internal controls, ethics and compliance programmes or measures adopted by enterprises in order to honour these commitments. Enterprises should also foster openness and dialogue with the public so as to promote its awareness of and co-operation with the fight against bribery, bribe solicitation and extortion.

6. Promote employee awareness of and compliance with company policies and internal controls, ethics and compliance programmes or measures against bribery, bribe solicitation and extortion through appropriate dissemination of such policies, programmes or measures and through training programmes and disciplinary procedures.

7. Not make illegal contributions to candidates for public office or to political parties or to other political organisations. Political contributions should fully comply with public disclosure requirements and should be reported to senior management.

Commentary on Combating Bribery, Bribe Solicitation and Extortion

74. Bribery and corruption are damaging to democratic institutions and the governance of corporations. They discourage investment and distort international competitive conditions. In particular, the diversion of funds through corrupt practices undermines attempts by citizens to achieve higher levels of economic, social and environmental welfare, and it impedes efforts to reduce poverty. Enterprises have an important role to play in combating these practices.

75. Propriety, integrity and transparency in both the public and private domains are key concepts in the fight against bribery, bribe solicitation and extortion. The business community, non-governmental organisations, governments and inter-governmental organisations have all co-operated to strengthen public support for anticorruption measures and to enhance transparency and public awareness of the problems of corruption and bribery. The adoption of appropriate corporate governance practices is also an essential element in fostering a culture of ethics within enterprises.

76. The *Convention on Combating Bribery of Foreign Public Officials in International Business Transactions* (the *Anti-Bribery Convention*) entered into force on 15 February 1999. The *Anti-Bribery Convention*, along with the *2009 Recommendation for Further Combating Bribery of Foreign Public Officials in International Business Transactions* (the *2009 Anti-Bribery Recommendation*), the *2009 Recommendation on Tax Measures for Further Combating Bribery of Foreign Public Officials in International Business Transactions*, and the *2006 Recommendation on Bribery and Officially Supported Export Credits*, are the core OECD instruments which target the offering side of the bribery transaction. They aim to eliminate the "supply" of bribes to foreign public officials, with each country taking responsibility for the activities of its enterprises and what happens within its own jurisdiction.[6] A programme of rigorous and systematic monitoring of countries' implementation of the Anti-Bribery Convention has been established to promote the full implementation of these instruments.

77. The 2009 *Anti-Bribery Recommendation* recommends in particular that governments encourage their enterprises to develop and adopt adequate internal controls, ethics and compliance programmes or measures for the purpose of preventing and detecting foreign bribery, taking into account the *Good Practice Guidance on Internal Controls, Ethics and*

6. For the purposes of the Convention, a "bribe" is defined as an "…offer, promise, or giv(ing) of any undue pecuniary or other advantage, whether directly or through intermediaries, to a foreign public official, for that official or for a third party, in order that the official act or refrain from acting in relation to the performance of official duties, in order to obtain or retain business or other improper advantage in the conduct of international business". The Commentaries to the Convention (paragraph 9) clarify that "small 'facilitation' payments do not constitute payments made 'to obtain or retain business or other improper advantage' within the meaning of paragraph 1 and, accordingly, are also not an offence. Such payments, which, in some countries, are made to induce public officials to perform their functions, such as issuing licenses or permits, are generally illegal in the foreign country concerned. Other countries can and should address this corrosive phenomenon by such means as support for programmes of good governance. …".

Compliance, included as Annex II to the *2009 Anti-Bribery Recommendation.* This *Good Practice Guidance* is addressed to enterprises as well as business organisations and professional associations, and highlights good practices for ensuring the effectiveness of their internal controls, ethics and compliance programmes or measures to prevent and detect foreign bribery.

78. Private sector and civil society initiatives also help enterprises to design and implement effective anti-bribery policies.

79. The *United Nations Convention against Corruption* (*UNCAC*), which entered into force on 14 December 2005, sets out a broad range of standards, measures and rules to fight corruption. Under the *UNCAC*, States Parties are required to prohibit their officials from receiving bribes and their enterprises from bribing domestic public officials, as well as foreign public officials and officials of public international organisations, and to consider disallowing private to private bribery. The *UNCAC* and the *Anti-Bribery Convention* are mutually supporting and complementary.

80. To address the demand side of bribery, good governance practices are important elements to prevent enterprises from being asked to pay bribes. Enterprises can support collective action initiatives on resisting bribe solicitation and extortion. Both home and host governments should assist enterprises confronted with solicitation of bribes and with extortion. The *Good Practice Guidance on Specific Articles of the Convention* in Annex I of the *2009 Anti-Bribery Recommendation* states that the *Anti-Bribery Convention* should be implemented in such a way that it does not provide a defence or exception where the foreign public official solicits a bribe. Furthermore, the *UNCAC* requires the criminalisation of bribe solicitation by domestic public officials.

VIII. Consumer Interests

When dealing with consumers, enterprises should act in accordance with fair business, marketing and advertising practices and should take all reasonable steps to ensure the quality and reliability of the goods and services that they provide. In particular, they should:

1. Ensure that the goods and services they provide meet all agreed or legally required standards for consumer health and safety, including those pertaining to health warnings and safety information.

2. Provide accurate, verifiable and clear information that is sufficient to enable consumers to make informed decisions, including information on the prices and, where appropriate, content, safe use, environmental attributes, maintenance, storage and disposal of goods and services. Where feasible this information should be provided in a manner that facilitates consumers' ability to compare products.

3. Provide consumers with access to fair, easy to use, timely and effective non-judicial dispute resolution and redress mechanisms, without unnecessary cost or burden.

4. Not make representations or omissions, nor engage in any other practices, that are deceptive, misleading, fraudulent or unfair.

5. Support efforts to promote consumer education in areas that relate to their business activities, with the aim of, *inter alia*, improving the ability of consumers to: *i)* make informed decisions involving complex goods, services and markets, *ii)* better understand the economic, environmental and social impact of their decisions and *iii)* support sustainable consumption.

6. Respect consumer privacy and take reasonable measures to ensure the security of personal data that they collect, store, process or disseminate.

7. Co-operate fully with public authorities to prevent and combat deceptive marketing practices (including misleading advertising and commercial fraud) and to diminish or prevent serious threats to public health and safety or to the environment deriving from the consumption, use or disposal of their goods and services.

8. Take into consideration, in applying the above principles, *i)* the needs of vulnerable and disadvantaged consumers and *ii)* the specific challenges that e-commerce may pose for consumers.

Commentary on Consumer Interests

81. The chapter on consumer interests of the OECD *Guidelines* for Multinational Enterprises draws on the work of the OECD Committee on Consumer Policy and the Committee on Financial Markets, as well as the work of other international organisations, including the International Chamber of Commerce, the International Organization for Standardization and the United Nations (*i.e.,* the *UN Guidelines on Consumer Policy*, as expanded in 1999).

82. The chapter recognises that consumer satisfaction and related interests constitute a fundamental basis for the successful operation of enterprises. It also recognises that consumer markets for goods and services have undergone major transformation over time. Regulatory reform, more open global markets, the development of new technologies and the growth in consumer services have been key agents of change, providing consumers with greater choice and the other benefits which derive from more open competition. At the same time, the pace of change and increased complexity of many markets have generally made it more difficult for consumers to compare and assess goods and services. Moreover, consumer demographics have also changed over time. Children are becoming increasingly significant forces in the market, as are the growing number of older adults. While consumers are better educated overall, many still lack the arithmetic and literacy skills that are required in today's more complex, information-intensive marketplace. Further, many consumers are increasingly interested in knowing the position and activities of enterprises on a broad range of economic, social and environmental issues, and in taking these into account when choosing goods and services.

83. The chapeau calls on enterprises to apply fair business, marketing and advertising practices and to ensure the quality and reliability of the products that they provide. These principles, it is noted, apply to both goods and services.

84. Paragraph 1 underscores the importance for enterprises to adhere to required health and safety standards and the importance for them to provide consumers with adequate health and safety information on their products.

85. Paragraph 2 concerns information disclosure. It calls for enterprises to provide information which is sufficient for consumers to make informed decisions. This would include information on the financial risks associated with products, where relevant. Furthermore, in some instances enterprises are legally required to provide information in a manner that enables consumers to make direct comparisons of goods and services (for example, unit pricing). In the absence of direct legislation, enterprises are encouraged to present information, when dealing with consumers, in a way that facilitates comparisons of goods and services and enables consumers to easily determine what the total cost of a product will be. It should be noted that what is considered to be "sufficient" can change over time and enterprises should be responsive to these changes. Any product and environmental claims that enterprises make should be based on adequate evidence and, as applicable, proper tests. Given consumers' growing interest in environmental issues and sustainable consumption, information should be provided, as appropriate, on the environmental attributes of products. This could include information on the energy efficiency and the degree of recyclability of products and, in the case of food products, information on agricultural practices.

86. Business conduct is increasingly considered by consumers when making their purchasing decisions. Enterprises are therefore encouraged to make information available on initiatives they have taken to integrate social and environmental concerns into their business operations and to otherwise support sustainable consumption. Chapter III of the *Guidelines* on Disclosure is relevant in this regard. Enterprises are there encouraged to communicate value statements or statements of business conduct to the public, including information on the social, ethical and environmental policies of the enterprise and other codes of conduct to which the company subscribes. Enterprises are encouraged to make this information available in plain language and in a format that is appealing to consumers. Growth in the number of enterprises reporting in these areas and targeting information to consumers would be welcome.

87. Paragraph 3 reflects language that is used in the 2007 Council *Recommendation on Consumer Dispute Resolution and Redress*. The Recommendation establishes a framework for developing effective approaches to address consumer complaints, including a series of actions that industry can take in this respect. It is noted that the mechanisms that many enterprises have established to resolve consumer disputes have helped increase consumer confidence and consumer satisfaction. These mechanisms can provide more practicable solutions to complaints than legal actions, which can be expensive, difficult and time consuming for all the parties involved. For these non-judicial

mechanisms to be effective, however, consumers need to be made aware of their existence and would benefit from guidance on how to file complaints, especially when claims involve cross-border or multi-dimensional transactions.

88. Paragraph 4 concerns deceptive, misleading, fraudulent and other unfair commercial practices. Such practices can distort markets, at the expense of both consumers and responsible enterprises and should be avoided.

89. Paragraph 5 concerns consumer education, which has taken on greater importance with the growing complexity of many markets and products. Governments, consumer organisations and many enterprises have recognised that this is a shared responsibility and that they can play important roles in this regard. The difficulties that consumers have experienced in evaluating complex products in financial and other areas have underscored the importance for stakeholders to work together to promote education aimed at improving consumer decision-making.

90. Paragraph 6 concerns personal data. The increasing collection and use of personal data by enterprises, fuelled in part by the Internet and technological advances, has highlighted the importance of protecting personal data against consumer privacy violations, including security breaches.

91. Paragraph 7 underscores the importance of enterprises to work with public authorities to help prevent and combat deceptive marketing practices more effectively. Co-operation is also called for to diminish or prevent threats to public health and safety and to the environment. This includes threats associated with the disposal of goods, as well as their consumption and use. This reflects recognition of the importance of considering the entire life-cycle of products.

92. Paragraph 8 calls on enterprises to take the situations of vulnerable and disadvantaged consumers into account when they market goods and services. Disadvantaged or vulnerable consumers refer to particular consumers or categories of consumers, who because of personal characteristics or circumstances (like age, mental or physical capacity, education, income, language or remote location) may meet particular difficulties in operating in today's information-intensive, globalised markets. The paragraph also highlights the growing importance of mobile and other forms of e-commerce in global markets. The benefits that such commerce provides are significant and growing. Governments have spent considerable time examining ways to ensure that consumers are afforded transparent and effective protection that is not less in the case of e-commerce than the level of protection afforded in more traditional forms of commerce.

IX. Science and Technology

Enterprises should:

1. Endeavour to ensure that their activities are compatible with the science and technology (S&T) policies and plans of the countries in which they operate and as appropriate contribute to the development of local and national innovative capacity.
2. Adopt, where practicable in the course of their business activities, practices that permit the transfer and rapid diffusion of technologies and know-how, with due regard to the protection of intellectual property rights.
3. When appropriate, perform science and technology development work in host countries to address local market needs, as well as employ host country personnel in an S&T capacity and encourage their training, taking into account commercial needs.
4. When granting licenses for the use of intellectual property rights or when otherwise transferring technology, do so on reasonable terms and conditions and in a manner that contributes to the long term sustainable development prospects of the host country.
5. Where relevant to commercial objectives, develop ties with local universities, public research institutions, and participate in co-operative research projects with local industry or industry associations.

Commentary on Science and Technology

93. In a knowledge-based and globalised economy where national borders matter less, even for small or domestically oriented enterprises, the ability to access and utilise technology and know-how is essential for improving enterprise performance. Such access is also important for the realisation of the economy-wide effects of technological progress, including productivity growth and job creation, within the context of sustainable development. Multinational enterprises are the main conduit of technology transfer across borders. They contribute to the national

innovative capacity of their host countries by generating, diffusing, and even enabling the use of new technologies by domestic enterprises and institutions. The R&D activities of MNEs, when well connected to the national innovation system, can help enhance the economic and social progress in their host countries. In turn, the development of a dynamic innovation system in the host country expands commercial opportunities for MNEs.

94. The chapter thus aims to promote, within the limits of economic feasibility, competitiveness concerns and other considerations, the diffusion by multinational enterprises of the fruits of research and development activities among the countries where they operate, contributing thereby to the innovative capacities of host countries. In this regard, fostering technology diffusion can include the commercialisation of products which imbed new technologies, licensing of process innovations, hiring and training of S&T personnel and development of R&D co-operative ventures. When selling or licensing technologies, not only should the terms and conditions negotiated be reasonable, but MNEs may want to consider the long-term developmental, environmental and other impacts of technologies for the home and host country. In their activities, multinational enterprises can establish and improve the innovative capacity of their international subsidiaries and subcontractors. In addition, MNEs can call attention to the importance of local scientific and technological infrastructure, both physical and institutional. In this regard, MNEs can usefully contribute to the formulation by host country governments of policy frameworks conducive to the development of dynamic innovation systems.

X. Competition

Enterprises should:

1. Carry out their activities in a manner consistent with all applicable competition laws and regulations, taking into account the competition laws of all jurisdictions in which the activities may have anti-competitive effects.

2. Refrain from entering into or carrying out anti-competitive agreements among competitors, including agreements to:

   a) fix prices;

   b) make rigged bids (collusive tenders);

   c) establish output restrictions or quotas; or

   d) share or divide markets by allocating customers, suppliers, territories or lines of commerce.

3. Co-operate with investigating competition authorities by, among other things and subject to applicable law and appropriate safeguards, providing responses as promptly and completely as practicable to requests for information, and considering the use of available instruments, such as waivers of confidentiality where appropriate, to promote effective and efficient co-operation among investigating authorities.

4. Regularly promote employee awareness of the importance of compliance with all applicable competition laws and regulations, and, in particular, train senior management of the enterprise in relation to competition issues.

Commentary on Competition

95. These recommendations emphasise the importance of competition laws and regulations to the efficient operation of both domestic and international markets and reaffirm the importance of compliance with

those laws and regulations by domestic and multinational enterprises. They also seek to ensure that all enterprises are aware of developments concerning the scope, remedies and sanctions of competition laws and the extent of co-operation among competition authorities. The term "competition" law is used to refer to laws, including both "antitrust" and "antimonopoly" laws, that variously prohibit: a) anti-competitive agreements; b) the abuse of market power or of dominance; c) the acquisition of market power or dominance by means other than efficient performance; or d) the substantial lessening of competition or the significant impeding of effective competition through mergers or acquisitions.

96. In general, competition laws and policies prohibit: a) hard core cartels; b) other anti-competitive agreements; c) anti-competitive conduct that exploits or extends market dominance or market power; and d) anti-competitive mergers and acquisitions. Under the 1998 Recommendation of the OECD Council Concerning Effective Action Against Hard Core Cartels, C(98)35/FINAL, the anticompetitive agreements referred to in sub a) constitute hard core cartels, but the Recommendation incorporates differences in member countries' laws, including differences in the laws' exemptions or provisions allowing for an exception or authorisation for activity that might otherwise be prohibited. The recommendations in these *Guidelines* do not suggest that enterprises should forego availing themselves of such legally available exemptions or provisions. The categories sub b) and c) are more general because the effects of other kinds of agreements and of unilateral conduct are more ambiguous, and there is less consensus on what should be considered anti-competitive.

97. The goal of competition policy is to contribute to overall welfare and economic growth by promoting market conditions in which the nature, quality, and price of goods and services are determined by competitive market forces. In addition to benefiting consumers and a jurisdiction's economy as a whole, such a competitive environment rewards enterprises that respond efficiently to consumer demand. Enterprises can contribute to this process by providing information and advice when governments are considering laws and policies that might reduce efficiency or otherwise reduce the competitiveness of markets.

98. Enterprises should be aware that competition laws continue to be enacted, and that it is increasingly common for those laws to prohibit anti-competitive activities that occur abroad if they have a harmful impact on domestic consumers. Moreover, cross-border trade and investment makes it more likely that anti-competitive conduct taking place in one jurisdiction will have harmful effects in other jurisdictions.

Enterprises should therefore take into account both the law of the country in which they are operating and the laws of all countries in which the effects of their conduct are likely to be felt.

99. Finally, enterprises should recognise that competition authorities are engaging in more and deeper co-operation in investigating and challenging anti-competitive activity. See generally: Recommendation of the Council Concerning Co-operation between Member Countries on Anticompetitive Practices Affecting International Trade, C(95)130/FINAL; Recommendation of the Council on Merger Review, C(2005)34. When the competition authorities of various jurisdictions are reviewing the same conduct, enterprises' facilitation of co-operation among the authorities promotes consistent and sound decision-making and competitive remedies while also permitting cost savings for governments and enterprises.

XI. Taxation

1. It is important that enterprises contribute to the public finances of host countries by making timely payment of their tax liabilities. In particular, enterprises should comply with both the letter and spirit of the tax laws and regulations of the countries in which they operate. Complying with the spirit of the law means discerning and following the intention of the legislature. It does not require an enterprise to make payment in excess of the amount legally required pursuant to such an interpretation. Tax compliance includes such measures as providing to the relevant authorities timely information that is relevant or required by law for purposes of the correct determination of taxes to be assessed in connection with their operations and conforming transfer pricing practices to the arm's length principle.

2. Enterprises should treat tax governance and tax compliance as important elements of their oversight and broader risk management systems. In particular, corporate boards should adopt tax risk management strategies to ensure that the financial, regulatory and reputational risks associated with taxation are fully identified and evaluated.

Commentary on Taxation

100. Corporate citizenship in the area of taxation implies that enterprises should comply with both the letter and the spirit of the tax laws and regulations in all countries in which they operate, co-operate with authorities and make information that is relevant or required by law available to them. An enterprise complies with the spirit of the tax laws and regulations if it takes reasonable steps to determine the intention of the legislature and interprets those tax rules consistent with that intention in light of the statutory language and relevant, contemporaneous legislative history. Transactions should not be structured in a way that will have tax results that are inconsistent with the underlying economic consequences of the transaction unless there exists specific legislation designed to give that result. In this case, the enterprise should reasonably believe that the transaction is structured in

a way that gives a tax result for the enterprise which is not contrary to the intentions of the legislature.

101. Tax compliance also entails co-operation with tax authorities and provision of the information they require to ensure an effective and equitable application of the tax laws. Such co-operation should include responding in a timely and complete manner to requests for information made by a competent authority pursuant to the provisions of a tax treaty or exchange of information agreement. However, this commitment to provide information is not without limitation. In particular, the *Guidelines* make a link between the information that should be provided and its relevance to the enforcement of applicable tax laws. This recognises the need to balance the burden on business in complying with applicable tax laws and the need for tax authorities to have the complete, timely and accurate information to enable them to enforce their tax laws.

102. Enterprises' commitments to co-operation, transparency and tax compliance should be reflected in risk management systems, structures and policies. In the case of enterprises having a corporate legal form, corporate boards are in a position to oversee tax risk in a number of ways. For example, corporate boards should proactively develop appropriate tax policy principles, as well as establish internal tax control systems so that the actions of management are consistent with the views of the board with regard to tax risk. The board should be informed about all potentially material tax risks and responsibility should be assigned for performing internal tax control functions and reporting to the board. A comprehensive risk management strategy that includes tax will allow the enterprise to not only act as a good corporate citizen but also to effectively manage tax risk, which can serve to avoid major financial, regulatory and reputation risk for an enterprise.

103. A member of a multinational enterprise group in one country may have extensive economic relationships with members of the same multinational enterprise group in other countries. Such relationships may affect the tax liability of each of the parties. Accordingly, tax authorities may need information from outside their jurisdiction in order to be able to evaluate those relationships and determine the tax liability of the member of the MNE group in their jurisdiction. Again, the information to be provided is limited to that which is relevant to or required by law for the proposed evaluation of those economic relationships for the purpose of determining the correct tax liability of the member of the MNE group. MNEs should co-operate in providing that information.

104. Transfer pricing is a particularly important issue for corporate citizenship and taxation. The dramatic increase in global trade and cross-border direct investment (and the important role played in such trade and investment by multinational enterprises) means that transfer pricing is a significant determinant of the tax liabilities of members of a multinational enterprise group because it materially influences the division of the tax base between countries in which the multinational enterprise operates. The arm's length principle which is included in both the OECD Model Tax Convention and the UN Model Double Taxation Convention between Developed and Developing Countries, is the internationally accepted standard for adjusting the profits between associated enterprises. Application of the arm's length principle avoids inappropriate shifting of profits or losses and minimises risks of double taxation. Its proper application requires multinational enterprises to co-operate with tax authorities and to furnish all information that is relevant or required by law regarding the selection of the transfer pricing method adopted for the international transactions undertaken by them and their related party. It is recognised that determining whether transfer pricing adequately reflects the arm's length standard (or principle) is often difficult both for multinational enterprises and for tax administrations and that its application is not an exact science.

105. The Committee on Fiscal Affairs of the OECD undertakes ongoing work to develop recommendations for ensuring that transfer pricing reflects the arm's length principle. Its work resulted in the publication in 1995 of the *OECD Transfer Pricing Guidelines for Multinational Enterprises and Tax Administrations* (*OECD Transfer Pricing Guidelines*) which was the subject of the Recommendation of the OECD Council on the Determination of Transfer Pricing between Associated Enterprises (members of an MNE group would normally fall within the definition of Associated Enterprises). The *OECD Transfer Pricing Guidelines* and that Council Recommendation are updated on an ongoing basis to reflect changes in the global economy and experiences of tax administrations and taxpayers dealing with transfer pricing. The arm's length principle as it applies to the attribution of profits of permanent establishments for the purposes of the determination of a host State's taxing rights under a tax treaty was the subject of an OECD Council Recommendation adopted in 2008.

106. The *OECD Transfer Pricing Guidelines* focus on the application of the arm's length principle to evaluate the transfer pricing of associated enterprises. The OECD Transfer Pricing *Guidelines* aim to help tax administrations (of both OECD member countries and non-member countries) and multinational enterprises by indicating mutually

satisfactory solutions to transfer pricing cases, thereby minimising conflict among tax administrations and between tax administrations and multinational enterprises and avoiding costly litigation. Multinational enterprises are encouraged to follow the guidance in the *OECD Transfer Pricing Guidelines*, as amended and supplemented[7], in order to ensure that their transfer prices reflect the arm's length principle.

7. One non-OECD adhering country, Brazil, does not apply the OECD *Transfer Pricing Guidelines* in its jurisdiction and accordingly the use of the guidance in those *Guidelines* by multinational enterprises for purposes of determining taxable income from their operations in this country does not apply in the light of the tax obligations set out in the legislation of this country. One other non-OECD adhering country, Argentina, points out that the *OECD Transfer Pricing Guidelines* are not compulsory in its jurisdiction.

Part II

Implementation Procedures of the OECD Guidelines for Multinational Enterprises

Amendment of the Decision of the Council on the OECD Guidelines for Multinational Enterprises

THE COUNCIL,

Having regard to the Convention on the Organisation for Economic Co-operation and Development of 14th December 1960;

Having regard to the OECD Declaration on International Investment and Multinational Enterprises (the "Declaration"), in which the Governments of adhering countries ("adhering countries") jointly recommend to multinational enterprises operating in or from their territories the observance of Guidelines for Multinational Enterprises (the "Guidelines");

Recognising that, since operations of multinational enterprises extend throughout the world, international co-operation on issues relating to the Declaration should extend to all countries;

Having regard to the Terms of Reference of the Investment Committee, in particular with respect to its responsibilities for the Declaration [C(84)171(Final), renewed in C/M(95)21];

Considering the Report on the First Review of the 1976 Declaration [C(79)102(Final)], the Report on the Second Review of the Declaration [C/MIN(84)5(Final)], the Report on the 1991 Review of the Declaration [DAFFE/IME(91)23], and the Report on the 2000 Review of the Guidelines [C(2000)96];

Having regard to the Second Revised Decision of the Council of June 1984 [C(84)90], amended June 1991 [C/MIN(91)7/ANN1] and repealed on 27 June 2000 [C(2000)96/FINAL];

Considering it desirable to enhance procedures by which consultations may take place on matters covered by these Guidelines and to promote the effectiveness of the Guidelines;

On the proposal of the Investment Committee:

DECIDES:

I. National Contact Points

1. Adhering countries shall set up National Contact Points to further the effectiveness of the *Guidelines* by undertaking promotional activities, handling enquiries and contributing to the resolution of issues that arise relating to the implementation of the *Guidelines* in specific instances, taking account of the attached procedural guidance. The business community, worker organisations, other non-governmental organisations and other interested parties shall be informed of the availability of such facilities.

2. National Contact Points in different countries shall co-operate if such need arises, on any matter related to the *Guidelines* relevant to their activities. As a general procedure, discussions at the national level should be initiated before contacts with other National Contact Points are undertaken.

3. National Contact Points shall meet regularly to share experiences and report to the Investment Committee.

4. Adhering countries shall make available human and financial resources to their National Contact Points so that they can effectively fulfil their responsibilities, taking into account internal budget priorities and practices.

II. The Investment Committee

1. The Investment Committee ("the Committee") shall periodically or at the request of an adhering country hold exchanges of views on matters covered by the *Guidelines* and the experience gained in their application.

2. The Committee shall periodically invite the Business and Industry Advisory Committee to the OECD (BIAC), and the Trade Union Advisory Committee to the OECD (TUAC) (the "advisory bodies"), OECD Watch, as well as other international partners to express their views on matters covered by the *Guidelines*. In addition, exchanges of views with them on these matters may be held at their request.

3. The Committee shall engage with non-adhering countries on matters covered by the *Guidelines* in order to promote responsible business conduct worldwide in accordance with the *Guidelines* and to create a level playing field. It shall also strive to co-operate with non-adhering countries that have a special interest in the *Guidelines* and in promoting their principles and standards.

4. The Committee shall be responsible for clarification of the *Guidelines*. Parties involved in a specific instance that gave rise to a request for clarification will be given the opportunity to express their views either orally or in writing. The Committee shall not reach conclusions on the conduct of individual enterprises.

5. The Committee shall hold exchanges of views on the activities of National Contact Points with a view to enhancing the effectiveness of the *Guidelines* and fostering functional equivalence of National Contact Points.

6. In fulfilling its responsibilities for the effective functioning of the *Guidelines*, the Committee shall take due account of the attached procedural guidance.

7. The Committee shall periodically report to the Council on matters covered by the *Guidelines*. In its reports, the Committee shall take account of reports by National Contact Points and the views expressed by the advisory bodies, OECD Watch, other international partners and non-adhering countries as appropriate.

8. The Committee shall, in co-operation with National Contact Points, pursue a proactive agenda that promotes the effective observance by enterprises of the principles and standards contained in the *Guidelines*. It shall, in particular, seek opportunities to collaborate with the advisory bodies, OECD Watch, other international partners and other stakeholders in order to encourage the positive contributions that multinational enterprises can make, in the context of the *Guidelines*, to economic, environmental and social progress with a view to achieving sustainable development, and to help them identify and respond to risks of adverse impacts associated with particular products, regions, sectors or industries.

III. Review of the Decision

This Decision shall be periodically reviewed. The Committee shall make proposals for this purpose.

Procedural Guidance

I. National Contact Points

The role of National Contact Points (NCPs) is to further the effectiveness of the *Guidelines*. NCPs will operate in accordance with core criteria of visibility, accessibility, transparency and accountability to further the objective of functional equivalence.

A. Institutional Arrangements

Consistent with the objective of functional equivalence and furthering the effectiveness of the *Guidelines*, adhering countries have flexibility in organising their NCPs, seeking the active support of social partners, including the business community, worker organisations, other non-governmental organisations, and other interested parties.

Accordingly, the National Contact Points:

1. Will be composed and organised such that they provide an effective basis for dealing with the broad range of issues covered by the *Guidelines* and enable the NCP to operate in an impartial manner while maintaining an adequate level of accountability to the adhering government.
2. Can use different forms of organisation to meet this objective. An NCP can consist of senior representatives from one or more Ministries, may be a senior government official or a government office headed by a senior official, be an interagency group, or one that contains independent experts. Representatives of the business community, worker organisations and other non-governmental organisations may also be included.
3. Will develop and maintain relations with representatives of the business community, worker organisations and other interested parties that are able to contribute to the effective functioning of the *Guidelines*.

B. Information and Promotion

The National Contact Point will:

1. Make the *Guidelines* known and available by appropriate means, including through on-line information, and in national languages. Prospective investors (inward and outward) should be informed about the *Guidelines*, as appropriate.

2. Raise awareness of the *Guidelines* and their implementation procedures, including through co-operation, as appropriate, with the business community, worker organisations, other non-governmental organisations, and the interested public.

3. Respond to enquiries about the *Guidelines* from:

    a) other National Contact Points;

    b) the business community, worker organisations, other non-governmental organisations and the public; and

    c) governments of non-adhering countries.

C. Implementation in Specific Instances

The National Contact Point will contribute to the resolution of issues that arise relating to implementation of the *Guidelines* in specific instances in a manner that is impartial, predictable, equitable and compatible with the principles and standards of the *Guidelines*. The NCP will offer a forum for discussion and assist the business community, worker organisations, other non-governmental organisations, and other interested parties concerned to deal with the issues raised in an efficient and timely manner and in accordance with applicable law. In providing this assistance, the NCP will:

1. Make an initial assessment of whether the issues raised merit further examination and respond to the parties involved.

2. Where the issues raised merit further examination, offer good offices to help the parties involved to resolve the issues. For this purpose, the NCP will consult with these parties and where relevant:

    a) seek advice from relevant authorities, and/or representatives of the business community, worker organisations, other non-governmental organisations, and relevant experts;

    b) consult the NCP in the other country or countries concerned;

    c) seek the guidance of the Committee if it has doubt about the interpretation of the *Guidelines* in particular circumstances;

d) offer, and with the agreement of the parties involved, facilitate access to consensual and non-adversarial means, such as conciliation or mediation, to assist the parties in dealing with the issues.

3. At the conclusion of the procedures and after consultation with the parties involved, make the results of the procedures publicly available, taking into account the need to protect sensitive business and other stakeholder information, by issuing:

   a) a statement when the NCP decides that the issues raised do not merit further consideration. The statement should at a minimum describe the issues raised and the reasons for the NCP's decision;

   b) a report when the parties have reached agreement on the issues raised. The report should at a minimum describe the issues raised, the procedures the NCP initiated in assisting the parties and when agreement was reached. Information on the content of the agreement will only be included insofar as the parties involved agree thereto;

   c) a statement when no agreement is reached or when a party is unwilling to participate in the procedures. This statement should at a minimum describe the issues raised, the reasons why the NCP decided that the issues raised merit further examination and the procedures the NCP initiated in assisting the parties. The NCP will make recommendations on the implementation of the *Guidelines* as appropriate, which should be included in the statement. Where appropriate, the statement could also include the reasons that agreement could not be reached.

The NCP will notify the results of its specific instance procedures to the Committee in a timely manner.

4. In order to facilitate resolution of the issues raised, take appropriate steps to protect sensitive business and other information and the interests of other stakeholders involved in the specific instance. While the procedures under paragraph 2 are underway, confidentiality of the proceedings will be maintained. At the conclusion of the procedures, if the parties involved have not agreed on a resolution of the issucs raised, they are free to communicate about and discuss these issues. However, information and views provided during the proceedings by another party involved will remain confidential, unless that other party agrees to their disclosure or this would be contrary to the provisions of national law.

5. If issues arise in non-adhering countries, take steps to develop an understanding of the issues involved, and follow these procedures where relevant and practicable.

D. Reporting

1. Each NCP will report annually to the Committee.
2. Reports should contain information on the nature and results of the activities of the NCP, including implementation activities in specific instances.

II. Investment Committee

1. The Committee will consider requests from NCPs for assistance in carrying out their activities, including in the event of doubt about the interpretation of the *Guidelines* in particular circumstances.

2. The Committee will, with a view to enhancing the effectiveness of the *Guidelines* and to fostering the functional equivalence of NCPs:

    a) consider the reports of NCPs;

    b) consider a substantiated submission by an adhering country, an advisory body or OECD Watch on whether an NCP is fulfilling its responsibilities with regard to its handling of specific instances;

    c) consider issuing a clarification where an adhering country, an advisory body or OECD Watch makes a substantiated submission on whether an NCP has correctly interpreted the *Guidelines* in specific instances;

    d) make recommendations, as necessary, to improve the functioning of NCPs and the effective implementation of the *Guidelines*;

    e) co-operate with international partners;

    f) engage with interested non-adhering countries on matters covered by the *Guidelines* and their implementation.

3. The Committee may seek and consider advice from experts on any matters covered by the *Guidelines*. For this purpose, the Committee will decide on suitable procedures.

4. The Committee will discharge its responsibilities in an efficient and timely manner.

5. In discharging its responsibilities, the Committee will be assisted by the OECD Secretariat, which, under the overall guidance of the Investment Committee, and subject to the Organisation's Programme of Work and Budget, will:

   a) serve as a central point of information for NCPs that have questions on the promotion and implementation of the *Guidelines*;

   b) collect and make publicly available relevant information on recent trends and emerging practices with regard to the promotional activities of NCPs and the implementation of the *Guidelines* in specific instances. The Secretariat will develop unified reporting formats to support the establishment and maintenance of an up-to-date database on specific instances and conduct regular analysis of these specific instances;

   c) facilitate peer learning activities, including voluntary peer evaluations, as well as capacity building and training, in particular for NCPs of new adhering countries, on the implementation procedures of the *Guidelines* such as promotion and the facilitation of conciliation and mediation;

   d) facilitate co-operation between NCPs where appropriate; and

   e) promote the *Guidelines* in relevant international forums and meetings and provide support to NCPs and the Committee in their efforts to raise awareness of the *Guidelines* among non-adhering countries.

Commentary on the Implementation Procedures of the OECD Guidelines for Multinational Enterprises

1. The Council Decision represents the commitment of adhering countries to further the implementation of the recommendations contained in the text of the *Guidelines*. Procedural guidance for both NCPs and the Investment Committee is attached to the Council Decision.

2. The Council Decision sets out key adhering country responsibilities for the *Guidelines* with respect to NCPs, summarised as follows:

   - Setting up NCPs (which will take account of the procedural guidance attached to the Decision), and informing interested parties of the availability of *Guidelines*-related facilities.
   - Making available necessary human and financial resources.
   - Enabling NCPs in different countries to co-operate with each other as necessary.
   - Enabling NCPs to meet regularly and report to the Committee.

3. The Council Decision also establishes the Committee's responsibilities for the *Guidelines*, including:

   - Organising exchanges of views on matters relating to the *Guidelines*.
   - Issuing clarifications as necessary.
   - Holding exchanges of views on the activities of NCPs.
   - Reporting to the OECD Council on the *Guidelines*.

4. The Investment Committee is the OECD body responsible for overseeing the functioning of the *Guidelines*. This responsibility applies not only to the *Guidelines*, but to all elements of the Declaration (National Treatment Instrument, and the instruments on International Investment Incentives and Disincentives, and Conflicting Requirements). The Committee seeks to ensure that each element in the Declaration is respected and understood, and that they all complement and operate in harmony with each other.

5. Reflecting the increasing relevance of responsible business conduct to countries outside the OECD, the Decision provides for engagement and co-operation with non-adhering countries on matters covered by the *Guidelines*. This provision allows the Committee to arrange special meetings with interested non-adhering countries to promote understanding of the standards and principles contained in the *Guidelines* and of their implementation procedures. Subject to relevant OECD procedures, the Committee may also associate them with special activities or projects on responsible business conduct, including by inviting them to its meetings and to the Corporate Responsibility Roundtables.

6. In its pursuit of a proactive agenda, the Committee will co-operate with NCPs and seek opportunities to collaborate with the advisory bodies, OECD Watch, and other international partners. Further guidance for NCPs in this respect is provided in paragraph 18.

I. Commentary on the Procedural Guidance for NCPs

7. National Contact Points have an important role in enhancing the profile and effectiveness of the *Guidelines*. While it is enterprises that are responsible for observing the *Guidelines* in their day-to-day behaviour, governments can contribute to improving the effectiveness of the implementation procedures. To this end, they have agreed that better guidance for the conduct and activities of NCPs is warranted, including through regular meetings and Committee oversight.

8. Many of the functions in the Procedural Guidance of the Decision are not new, but reflect experience and recommendations developed over the years. By making them explicit the expected functioning of the implementation mechanisms of the *Guidelines* is made more transparent. All functions are now outlined in four parts of the Procedural Guidance pertaining to NCPs: institutional arrangements, information and promotion, implementation in specific instances, and reporting.

9. These four parts are preceded by an introductory paragraph that sets out the basic purpose of NCPs, together with core criteria to promote the concept of "functional equivalence". Since governments are accorded flexibility in the way they organise NCPs, NCPs should function in a visible, accessible, transparent, and accountable manner. These criteria will guide NCPs in carrying out their activities and will also assist the Committee in discussing the conduct of NCPs.

Core Criteria for Functional Equivalence in the Activities of NCPs

Visibility. In conformity with the Decision, adhering governments agree to nominate NCPs, and also to inform the business community, worker organisations and other interested parties, including NGOs, about the availability of facilities associated with NCPs in the implementation of the *Guidelines*. Governments are expected to publish information about their NCPs and to take an active role in promoting the *Guidelines*, which could include hosting seminars and meetings on the instrument. These events could be arranged in co-operation with business, labour, NGOs, and other interested parties, though not necessarily with all groups on each occasion.

Accessibility. Easy access to NCPs is important to their effective functioning. This includes facilitating access by business, labour, NGOs, and other members of the public. Electronic communications can also assist in this regard. NCPs would respond to all legitimate requests for information, and also undertake to deal with specific issues raised by parties concerned in an efficient and timely manner.

Transparency. Transparency is an important criterion with respect to its contribution to the accountability of the NCP and in gaining the confidence of the general public. Thus, as a general principle, the activities of the NCP will be transparent. Nonetheless when the NCP offers its "good offices" in implementing the *Guidelines* in specific instances, it will be in the interests of their effectiveness to take appropriate steps to establish confidentiality of the proceedings. Outcomes will be transparent unless preserving confidentiality is in the best interests of effective implementation of the *Guidelines*.

Accountability. A more active role with respect to enhancing the profile of the *Guidelines* – and their potential to aid in the management of difficult issues between enterprises and the societies in which they operate – will also put the activities of NCPs in the public eye. Nationally, parliaments could have a role to play. Annual reports and regular meetings of NCPs will provide an opportunity to share experiences and encourage "best practices" with respect to NCPs. The Committee will also hold exchanges of views, where experiences would be exchanged and the effectiveness of the activities of NCPs could be assessed.

Institutional Arrangements

10. NCP leadership should be such that it retains the confidence of social partners and other stakeholders, and fosters the public profile of the *Guidelines*.

11. Regardless of the structure Governments have chosen for their NCP, they can also establish multi-stakeholder advisory or oversight bodies to assist NCPs in their tasks.

12. NCPs, whatever their composition, are expected to develop and maintain relations with representatives of the business community, worker organisations, other non-governmental organisations, and other interested parties.

Information and Promotion

13. The NCP functions associated with information and promotion are fundamentally important to enhancing the profile of the *Guidelines*.

14. NCPs are required to make the *Guidelines* better known and available online and by other appropriate means, including in national languages. English and French language versions will be available from the OECD, and website links to the *Guidelines* website are encouraged. As appropriate, NCPs will also provide prospective investors, both inward and outward, with information about the *Guidelines*.

15. NCPs should provide information on the procedures that parties should follow when raising or responding to a specific instance. It should include advice on the information that is necessary to raise a specific instance, the requirements for parties participating in specific instances, including confidentiality, and the processes and indicative timeframes that will be followed by the NCP.

16. In their efforts to raise awareness of the *Guidelines*, NCPs will co-operate with a wide variety of organisations and individuals, including, as appropriate, the business community, worker organisations, other non-governmental organisations, and other interested parties. Such organisations have a strong stake in the promotion of the *Guidelines* and their institutional networks provide opportunities for promotion that, if used for this purpose, will greatly enhance the efforts of NCPs in this regard.

17. Another basic activity expected of NCPs is responding to legitimate enquiries. Three groups have been singled out for attention in this regard: *i)* other NCPs (reflecting a provision in the Decision); *ii)* the business community, worker organisations, other non-governmental organisations and the public; and *iii)* governments of non-adhering countries.

Proactive Agenda

18. In accordance with the Investment Committee's proactive agenda, NCPs should maintain regular contact, including meetings, with social partners and other stakeholders in order to:

    a) consider new developments and emerging practices concerning responsible business conduct;

    b) support the positive contributions enterprises can make to economic, social and environmental progress;

    c) participate where appropriate in collaborative initiatives to identify and respond to risks of adverse impacts associated with particular products, regions, sectors or industries.

Peer Learning

19. In addition to contributing to the Committee's work to enhance the effectiveness of the *Guidelines*, NCPs will engage in joint peer learning activities. In particular, they are encouraged to engage in horizontal, thematic peer reviews and voluntary NCP peer evaluations. Such peer learning can be carried out through meetings at the OECD or through direct co-operation between NCPs.

Implementation in Specific Instances

20. When issues arise relating to implementation of the *Guidelines* in specific instances, the NCP is expected to help resolve them. This section of the Procedural Guidance provides guidance to NCPs on how to handle specific instances.

21. The effectiveness of the specific instances procedure depends on good faith behaviour of all parties involved in the procedures. Good faith behaviour in this context means responding in a timely fashion, maintaining confidentiality where appropriate, refraining from misrepresenting the process and from threatening or taking reprisals against parties involved in the procedure, and genuinely engaging in the procedures with a view to finding a solution to the issues raised in accordance with the *Guidelines*.

Guiding Principles for Specific Instances

22. Consistent with the core criteria for functional equivalence in their activities NCPs should deal with specific instances in a manner that is:

Impartial. NCPs should ensure impartiality in the resolution of specific instances.

Predictable. NCPs should ensure predictability by providing clear and publicly available information on their role in the resolution of specific instances, including the provision of good offices, the stages of the specific instance process including indicative timeframes, and the potential role they can play in monitoring the implementation of agreements reached between the parties.

Equitable. NCPs should ensure that the parties can engage in the process on fair and equitable terms, for example by providing reasonable access to sources of information relevant to the procedure.

Compatible with the Guidelines. NCPs should operate in accordance with the principles and standards contained in the *Guidelines*.

Coordination between NCPs in Specific Instances

23. Generally, issues will be dealt with by the NCP of the country in which the issues have arisen. Among adhering countries, such issues will first be discussed on the national level and, where appropriate, pursued at the bilateral level. The NCP of the host country should consult with the NCP of the home country in its efforts to assist the parties in resolving the issues. The NCP of the home country should strive to provide appropriate assistance in a timely manner when requested by the NCP of the host country.

24. When issues arise from an enterprise's activity that takes place in several adhering countries or from the activity of a group of enterprises organised as consortium, joint venture or other similar form, based in different adhering countries, the NCPs involved should consult with a view to agreeing on which NCP will take the lead in assisting the parties. The NCPs can seek assistance from the Chair of the Investment Committee in arriving at such agreement. The lead NCP should consult with the other NCPs, which should provide appropriate assistance when requested by the lead NCP. If the parties fail to reach an agreement, the lead NCP should make a final decision in consultation with the other NCPs.

Initial Assessment

25. In making an initial assessment of whether the issue raised merits further examination, the NCP will need to determine whether the issue is

bona fide and relevant to the implementation of the *Guidelines*. In this context, the NCP will take into account:

- the identity of the party concerned and its interest in the matter.
- whether the issue is material and substantiated.
- whether there seems to be a link between the enterprise's activities and the issue raised in the specific instance.
- the relevance of applicable law and procedures, including court rulings.
- how similar issues have been, or are being, treated in other domestic or international proceedings.
- whether the consideration of the specific issue would contribute to the purposes and effectiveness of the *Guidelines*.

26. When assessing the significance for the specific instance procedure of other domestic or international proceedings addressing similar issues in parallel, NCPs should not decide that issues do not merit further consideration solely because parallel proceedings have been conducted, are under way or are available to the parties concerned. NCPs should evaluate whether an offer of good offices could make a positive contribution to the resolution of the issues raised and would not create serious prejudice for either of the parties involved in these other proceedings or cause a contempt of court situation. In making such an evaluation, NCPs could take into account practice among other NCPs and, where appropriate, consult with the institutions in which the parallel proceeding is being or could be conducted. Parties should also assist NCPs in their consideration of these matters by providing relevant information on the parallel proceedings.

27. Following its initial assessment, the NCP will respond to the parties concerned. If the NCP decides that the issue does not merit further consideration, it will inform the parties of the reasons for its decision.

Providing Assistance to the Parties

28. Where the issues raised merit further consideration, the NCP would discuss the issue further with parties involved and offer "good offices" in an effort to contribute informally to the resolution of issues. Where relevant, NCPs will follow the procedures set out in paragraph C-2a) through C-2d). This could include seeking the advice of relevant authorities, as well as representatives of the business community, labour organisations, other non-governmental organisations, and experts.

Consultations with NCPs in other countries, or seeking guidance on issues related to the interpretation of the *Guidelines* may also help to resolve the issue.

29. As part of making available good offices, and where relevant to the issues at hand, NCPs will offer, or facilitate access to, consensual and non-adversarial procedures, such as conciliation or mediation, to assist in dealing with the issues at hand. In common with accepted practices on conciliation and mediation procedures, these procedures would be used only upon agreement of the parties concerned and their commitment to participate in good faith during the procedure.

30. When offering their good offices, NCPs may take steps to protect the identity of the parties involved where there are strong reasons to believe that the disclosure of this information would be detrimental to one or more of the parties. This could include circumstances where there may be a need to withhold the identity of a party or parties from the enterprise involved.

Conclusion of the Procedures

31. NCPs are expected to always make the results of a specific instance publicly available in accordance with paragraphs C-3 and C-4 of the Procedural Guidance.

32. When the NCP, after having carried out its initial assessment, decides that the issues raised in the specific instance do not merit further consideration, it will make a statement publicly available after consultations with the parties involved and taking into account the need to preserve the confidentiality of sensitive business and other information. If the NCP believes that, based on the results of its initial assessment, it would be unfair to publicly identify a party in a statement on its decision, it may draft the statement so as to protect the identity of the party.

33. The NCP may also make publicly available its decision that the issues raised merit further examination and its offer of good offices to the parties involved.

34. If the parties involved reach agreement on the issues raised, the parties should address in their agreement how and to what extent the content of the agreement is to be made publicly available. The NCP, in consultation with the parties, will make publicly available a report with the results of the proceedings. The parties may also agree to seek the assistance of the NCP in following-up on the implementation of the

agreement and the NCP may do so on terms agreed between the parties and the NCP.

35. If the parties involved fail to reach agreement on the issues raised or if the NCP finds that one or more of the parties to the specific instance is unwilling to engage or to participate in good faith, the NCP will issue a statement, and make recommendations as appropriate, on the implementation of the *Guidelines*. This procedure makes it clear that an NCP will issue a statement, even when it feels that a specific recommendation is not called for. The statement should identify the parties concerned, the issues involved, the date on which the issues were raised with the NCP, any recommendations by the NCP, and any observations the NCP deems appropriate to include on the reasons why the proceedings did not produce an agreement.

36. The NCP should provide an opportunity for the parties to comment on a draft statement. However, the statement is that of the NCP and it is within the NCP's discretion to decide whether to change the draft statement in response to comments from the parties. If the NCP makes recommendations to the parties, it may be appropriate under specific circumstances for the NCP to follow-up with the parties on their response to these recommendations. If the NCP deems it appropriate to follow-up on its recommendations, the timeframe for doing so should be addressed in the statement of the NCP.

37. Statements and reports on the results of the proceedings made publicly available by the NCPs could be relevant to the administration of government programmes and policies. In order to foster policy coherence, NCPs are encouraged to inform these government agencies of their statements and reports when they are known by the NCP to be relevant to a specific agency's policies and programmes. This provision does not change the voluntary nature of the *Guidelines*.

Transparency and Confidentiality

38. Transparency is recognised as a general principle for the conduct of NCPs in their dealings with the public (see paragraph 9 in "Core Criteria" section, above). However, paragraph C-4 of the Procedural Guidance recognises that there are specific circumstances where confidentiality is important. The NCP will take appropriate steps to protect sensitive business information. Equally, other information, such as the identity of individuals involved in the procedures, should be kept confidential in the interests of the effective implementation of the *Guidelines*. It is understood that proceedings include the facts and arguments brought forward by the parties. Nonetheless, it remains

important to strike a balance between transparency and confidentiality in order to build confidence in the *Guidelines* procedures and to promote their effective implementation. Thus, while paragraph C-4 broadly outlines that the proceedings associated with implementation will normally be confidential, the results will normally be transparent.

Issues Arising in Non-Adhering Countries

39. As noted in paragraph 2 of the Concepts and Principles chapter, enterprises are encouraged to observe the *Guidelines* wherever they operate, taking into account the particular circumstances of each host country.

- In the event that *Guidelines*-related issues arise in a non-adhering country, home NCPs will take steps to develop an understanding of the issues involved. While it may not always be practicable to obtain access to all pertinent information, or to bring all the parties involved together, the NCP may still be in a position to pursue enquiries and engage in other fact finding activities. Examples of such steps could include contacting the management of the enterprise in the home country, and, as appropriate, embassies and government officials in the non-adhering country.

- Conflicts with host country laws, regulations, rules and policies may make effective implementation of the *Guidelines* in specific instances more difficult than in adhering countries. As noted in the commentary to the General Policies chapter, while the *Guidelines* extend beyond the law in many cases, they should not and are not intended to place an enterprise in a situation where it faces conflicting requirements.

- The parties involved will have to be advised of the limitations inherent in implementing the *Guidelines* in non-adhering countries.

- Issues relating to the *Guidelines* in non-adhering countries could also be discussed at NCP meetings with a view to building expertise in handling issues arising in non-adhering countries.

Indicative Timeframe

40. The specific instance procedure comprises three different stages:

1. *Initial assessment and decision whether to offer good offices to assist the parties*: NCPs should seek to conclude an initial assessment

within three months, although additional time might be needed in order to collect information necessary for an informed decision.

2. *Assistance to the parties in their efforts to resolve the issues raised*: If an NCP decides to offer its good offices, it should strive to facilitate the resolution of the issues in a timely manner. Recognising that progress through good offices, including mediation and conciliation, ultimately depends upon the parties involved, the NCP should, after consultation with the parties, establish a reasonable timeframe for the discussion between the parties to resolve the issues raised. If they fail to reach an agreement within this timeframe, the NCP should consult with the parties on the value of continuing its assistance to the parties; if the NCP comes to the conclusion that the continuation of the procedure is not likely to be productive, it should conclude the process and proceed to prepare a statement.

3. *Conclusion of the procedures*: The NCP should issue its statement or report within three months after the conclusion of the procedure.

41. As a general principle, NCPs should strive to conclude the procedure within 12 months from receipt of the specific instance. It is recognised that this timeframe may need to be extended if circumstances warrant it, such as when the issues arise in a non-adhering country.

Reporting to the Investment Committee

42. Reporting would be an important responsibility of NCPs that would also help to build up a knowledge base and core competencies in furthering the effectiveness of the *Guidelines*. In this light, NCPs will report to the Investment Committee in order to include in the Annual Report on the OECD *Guidelines* information on all specific instances that have been initiated by parties, including those that are in the process of an initial assessment, those for which offers of good offices have been extended and discussions are in progress, and those in which the NCP has decided not to extend an offer of good offices after an initial assessment. In reporting on implementation activities in specific instances, NCPs will comply with transparency and confidentiality considerations as set out in paragraph C-4.

II. Commentary on the Procedural Guidance for the Investment Committee

43. The Procedural Guidance to the Council Decision provides additional guidance to the Committee in carrying out its responsibilities, including:

    - Discharging its responsibilities in an efficient and timely manner.
    - Considering requests from NCPs for assistance.
    - Holding exchanges of views on the activities of NCPs.
    - Providing for the possibility of seeking advice from international partners and experts.

44. The non-binding nature of the *Guidelines* precludes the Committee from acting as a judicial or quasi-judicial body. Nor should the findings and statements made by the NCP (other than interpretations of the *Guidelines*) be questioned by a referral to the Committee. The provision that the Committee shall not reach conclusions on the conduct of individual enterprises has been maintained in the Decision itself.

45. The Committee will consider requests from NCPs for assistance, including in the event of doubt about the interpretation of the *Guidelines* in particular circumstances. This paragraph reflects paragraph C-2c) of the Procedural Guidance to the Council Decision pertaining to NCPs, where NCPs are invited to seek the guidance of the Committee if they have doubt about the interpretation of the *Guidelines* in these circumstances.

46. When discussing NCP activities, the Committee may make recommendations, as necessary, to improve their functioning, including with respect to the effective implementation of the *Guidelines*.

47. A substantiated submission by an adhering country, an advisory body or OECD Watch that an NCP was not fulfilling its procedural responsibilities in the implementation of the *Guidelines* in specific instances will also be considered by the Committee. This complements provisions in the section of the Procedural Guidance pertaining to NCPs reporting on their activities.

48. Clarifications of the meaning of the *Guidelines* at the multilateral level would remain a key responsibility of the Committee to ensure that the meaning of the *Guidelines* would not vary from country to country. A substantiated submission by an adhering country, an advisory body or OECD Watch with respect to whether an NCP interpretation of the

Guidelines is consistent with Committee interpretations will also be considered.

49. In order to engage with non-adhering countries on matters covered by the *Guidelines*, the Committee may invite interested non-adhering countries to its meetings, annual Roundtables on Corporate Responsibility, and meetings relating to specific projects on responsible business conduct.

50. Finally, the Committee may wish to call on experts to address and report on broader issues (for example, child labour or human rights) or individual issues, or to improve the effectiveness of procedures. For this purpose, the Committee could call on OECD in-house expertise, international organisations, the advisory bodies, non-governmental organisations, academics and others. It is understood that this will not become a panel to settle individual issues.

ORGANISATION FOR ECONOMIC CO-OPERATION AND DEVELOPMENT

The OECD is a unique forum where governments work together to address the economic, social and environmental challenges of globalisation. The OECD is also at the forefront of efforts to understand and to help governments respond to new developments and concerns, such as corporate governance, the information economy and the challenges of an ageing population. The Organisation provides a setting where governments can compare policy experiences, seek answers to common problems, identify good practice and work to co-ordinate domestic and international policies.

The OECD member countries are: Australia, Austria, Belgium, Canada, Chile, the Czech Republic, Denmark, Estonia, Finland, France, Germany, Greece, Hungary, Iceland, Ireland, Israel, Italy, Japan, Korea, Luxembourg, Mexico, the Netherlands, New Zealand, Norway, Poland, Portugal, the Slovak Republic, Slovenia, Spain, Sweden, Switzerland, Turkey, the United Kingdom and the United States. The European Union takes part in the work of the OECD.

OECD Publishing disseminates widely the results of the Organisation's statistics gathering and research on economic, social and environmental issues, as well as the conventions, guidelines and standards agreed by its members.

OECD PUBLISHING, 2, rue André-Pascal, 75775 PARIS CEDEX 16
(20 2011 10 1 P) ISBN 978-92-64-11528-6 – No. 58231 2011-01